AROUND THE BAY

ALL AROUND THE BAY

A Shoreline Guide to San Francisco Bay

Ruth A. Jackson

Chronicle Books □ San Francisco

Library of Congress Cataloging in Publication Data

Jackson, Ruth A.
    All around the Bay.

    Includes index.
1. San Francisco Bay Area (Calif.)—Description and
travel—Guide-books. I. Title.
F868.S156J33   1987   917.94'60453   87-6597
ISBN 0-87701-387-X (pbk.)

Editing: Deborah Stone
Typography: TBH/Typecast, Inc.
Book and Cover Design: Fearn Cutler
Cover Photograph: Baron Wolman

Photo credits:
All photographs by the author except the following:
Edna Bullock: 12, 74, 81
Richard Frear: 14, 21, 28
John R. Harris: 76
Pacific Aerial Surveys: 2

10 9 8 7 6 5 4 3 2 1

Chronicle Books
One Hallidie Plaza
San Francisco, CA 94102

CONTENTS

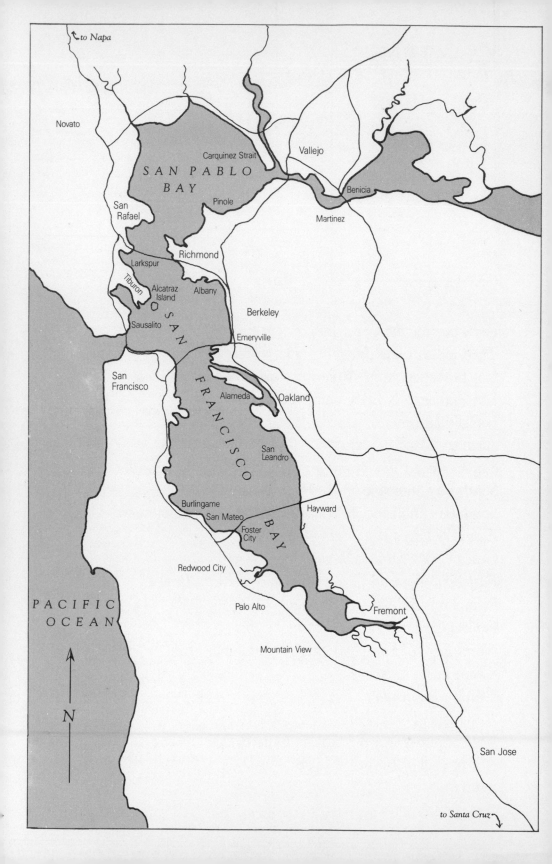

REDISCOVERING
the GREAT BAY of SAN FRANCISCO

Preface

San Francisco Bay is an irreplaceable gift of nature for all creatures who live near its shores. It is one of the wonders of the world, both for its beauty and its size.

When weary members of Gaspar de Portola's expedition (the Bay's official dis-coverers), stumbled on to its southern end in 1769, the Bay was larger and more beautiful.

In 1775 Juan Baptista de Anza's party, hoping to found a mission, climbed a flower-covered bluff overlooking the Bay and Father Pedro Font, the chaplain, called this great body of water "a marvel of nature" and "the harbor of harbors." He noted that from this mesa,

> one sees a large part of the port and its islands . . . and of the sea all that the sight can take in as far as beyond the Farallones. Although in my travels I saw very good sites and beautiful country, I saw none that pleased me as much as this. And I think that if it could be well settled like Europe, there would not be anything more beautiful in this world.

From earlier Indian eras to now, the Bay has meant many things to many people. Today windsurfers to yachtsmen to ship captains appreciate it as one of the world's largest harbors.

How large is the Bay? Its 558 square miles (including tidal marshes) stretch from the tip of the South Bay north and east to Chipps Island on Suisun Bay. Add the Sacramento and San Joaquin deltas, and it's 1,100 square miles larger—and will be bigger yet if the Bay's mean water level rises four feet within the next century, as some scientists predict.

Impressive as its size is, the Bay's most valuable asset may be its beauty, accessible to all who pause to look. The ever-changing ballet of light and fog, and the cobweb of bridges keep adjectives flowing and cameras clicking. Where else can you look up from your kitchen sink to catch a white cruise ship slipping out under the Golden

Opposite: The great Bay of San Francisco, 558 square miles of wildlife and recreation.

Gate, or dutifully jog along a Bayside bluff in the invigorating air while pelicans fly by at eye level, so close you feel their wing beat, or—locked in bumper to bumper traffic—count white egrets stationed along the shore?

It's refreshing to realize that humans aren't the only species to enjoy the Bay's bounty. Since it's on the flyway, millions of birds pause to rest and feed, from Vs of honking geese to migrating hawks and falcons. And wild places remain where you can meet deer and perhaps glimpse the bobcat or mountain lion. Also, since two major rivers and many other rivers, creeks, and sloughs flow in, bringing fresh water to mingle with the open sea water and marshes, 100 species of fish—both fresh water and ocean—make this their home. The result? Sport fishing can be exciting and you can bring home a big catch.

Another given is that you can enjoy the Bay's magic all year. Here the change of seasons is subtle. The weather may change more in a day or week than in a year. True, from November into March it does rain off and on. Even then you can enjoy the spectacle. Sitting by a window in a Sausalito restaurant, you might see seagulls gorging themselves during a herring run or harbor seals gazing back at you with curiosity. Warm and protected in your car at Fort Point, you can watch tons of sea water—over a million and a half acre-feet—surge in and out through the Golden Gate twice each day during the two- to nine-foot rise of the tides. Then there are those occasional winter days so balmy you catch spring fever. When that happens, leave your work, and go to it!

Fog? Yes, but it's not a four-letter word if you've remembered to bring a sweater. Fog can be beautiful, adding a dreamlike, muted quality to sharp edges. Notice how many scenic postcards of San Francisco feature tendrils, clouds, or banks of fog as it's pulled inland through the Gate by the intense heat of the valleys. When summer comes, most residents of the Bay's nine surrounding counties welcome the mournful blast of foghorns, for fog turns the Bay into a giant air conditioner, tempering heat and cold.

If you insist on sunshine, just wait. The gray often turns to gold and blue by noon. Also, if you travel a short distance inland the sun may be shining. Scattered throughout this book are tips on times and locations where the sun and Bay breezes are more likely to cooperate.

San Francisco Bay is 40 percent smaller than it was during the 5,000 or so years that Indians lived, undisturbed, near its edges. In 1850 marshlands bordering the Bay covered some 300 square miles. Unrelentingly noisy, smoke-belching industries, railroad tracks, sewage plants, and garbage dumps began to rim the 1,000 miles of Bay edges.

Then, especially in the mid-sixties, developers became the "economic good guys." They and local governments "reclaimed" an average of 2,300 acres a year until only about 75 square miles remained. After all, the birds, fish, and wildlife that depended on marshes for survival had no vote. But the tide of public awareness turned.

Spearheaded by public organizations like the Save San Francisco Bay Association, in 1965 the Bay Conservation and Development Commission (BCDC) became the first coastal management agency in the nation. Its goals were (and still are) to protect the Bay as a great natural resource for the benefit of present and future generations and to develop the Bay and its shoreline to their highest potential with a minimum of Bay filling.

When the BCDC took over, the public was officially welcome along only 4 miles of the 1,000 miles of Bay shoreline. Now more than 100 miles are open to public access, thanks also to military establishments, private holdings (and to garbage dumps, too) that kept at least some developers from bringing in bulldozers.

The battle for a clean, beautiful Bay that welcomes the public isn't over yet. Toxic wastes still endanger shellfish, fish, birds—and, subsequently, man. Air pollution can still color and choke the sky, especially in the South Bay and the northern edge of Contra Costa County. Yet pile worms, clams, and some species of fish are starting to return. And every few months new public fishing piers or more shoreline parks are built so you can "get away by the Bay," hear the swish of waves, breathe sea-washed air, and watch winged wildlife.

Besides hiking, bicycling, picnicking, or just plain gazing, world-famous complexes await your wallet if you're addicted to shopping. Restaurants? They vary from four-star Meccas to little known cafes on roads less traveled by. Then there are the Bay's "islands in time" to explore, some complete with historical buildings and fortifications. As for water-oriented sports, take your pick of dozens in addition to fishing, boating, and swimming. Many, like sandcastle building contests, are geared for children. And you don't have to go great distances; your goal is probably minutes away.

Whatever you prefer, if it's legal, you'll probably find it in these pages. So that you can locate your brand of recreation easily, most are in bold face. Use the index as a guide, then choose a portion of our great Bay of San Francisco to rediscover and enjoy. Whatever you pick won't be far away, whether you drive or take public transportation.

The shy harbor seal is just one of the wild creatures you'll see around the Bay.

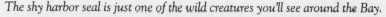

But times change. Although listings were checked right up to press time, you may discover that the "find" of a restaurant has changed cooks, the telephone number is different, or that the Victorian house you wanted to see has been demolished. I hope such incidents will be rare and suffered with understanding.

Ruth A. Jackson

Picnickers enjoy the views from atop Angel Island, in the center of the Bay.

THE GOLDEN GATE BRIDGE

The Golden Gate Bridge

The 6,450-foot **Golden Gate Bridge** that soars across the turbulent waters at the entry to San Francisco Bay is considered an engineering miracle. Its suspension span of 4,200 feet is no longer the world's longest. But this bridge by the Golden Gate must be the most beautiful, truly equal to its incomparable site.

In the toll-plaza parking lot at the span's south end, the statue of Joseph B. Strauss, chief engineer from 1929 to its opening in 1937, stands—usually festooned with tourists. A plaque extolls Strauss for "the eternal rainbow that he conceived and set into form."

Nearby is a cutout sample of one cable. You see the 27,572 wires it contains and try to comprehend that 80,000 miles of similar cable, weighing 24,500 tons, hold up the bridge, like a giant hammock, from 756-foot high towers. For a dramatic closeup of Bridge and Bay, climb the wooden steps behind the statue. For other views that change at each turn, take the Battery East trail that starts down towards Fort Point, turn west, and continue under the bridge.

You can, of course, quickly glimpse the spectacle driving over on Highway 101 (tolls are collected going south towards San Francisco). Better yet, during daylight hours why not bicycle or don comfortable shoes and a windbreaker and stroll from one vista point to the other? You'll enjoy the sweep of Bay and ocean more and have a bonus thrill when graceful sailboats and huge liners pass right under you.

Since metered parking at the toll-plaza is limited, consider taking Muni bus #28 or the Golden Gate Transit #64 there. Then you can savor the sights at your leisure. Another way to see the bridge is to find a friend with a boat or take one of the harbor cruises mentioned on page 21. When you pass underneath this great span linking San Francisco and Marin County, you'll feel respect, even awe, for the men who built it half a century ago.

Crossing on foot you'll feel the "give" of this flexible bridge where winds may blow the roadway many feet up and down and back and forth. Don't worry unduly unless it's midwinter. The span has been closed only three times due to violent storms: in 1951, 1982, and 1983—all in December. It's kept in shape by constant work, and a crew of thirty continually sandblasts and repaints it with a highly visible international orange—not gold—paint.

Eleven workers lost their lives during the bridge's construction and, since it opened, over 800 suicide-prone people have jumped over the side. Only a handful survived. Should a suicide-prevention barrier be built? Arguments have raged for years. One argument against it is that the barrier might interfere with the views. And that, many people, from residents to visitors, feel might interfere with magic.

View of the Golden Gate Bridge from Lands End.

SAN FRANCISCO NORTH WATERFRONT NEAR the GOLDEN GATE

Fort Point

Once you have driven—or, better yet, walked—across the Golden Gate Bridge, you understand why its soaring beauty has kept writers, artists, and photographers busy for decades. Another highlight, with the added seasoning of history, is **Fort Point** at the south end, under the bridge's mammoth girders.

The low-level views from the fort's seawall are impressive and it's exhilarating to watch surging two- to seven-foot tides rush in and out of this narrow, windy gate between Bay and ocean. Waves often pound against the rocky shore so close you get a tingling shower as you watch the comings and goings of ships and fog. An occasional whale (like the beloved Humphrey in 1985) turns in for a brief stay. You may also see and hear sea lions wave-surfing or diving for fish just off shore. You can try **fishing** yourself off the seawall or from the decrepit old pier, where **crabbing** is also often good.

Nothing remains of the rain-plagued adobe fort the Spanish built in 1794 on a high white cliff above this site. In 1853 the U.S. Army Corps of Engineers leveled both the old fort and the hill. The present Fort Point was completed in 1861, in time for the Civil War, with brick walls five to twelve feet thick and a huge tiered inside court. Then it bristled with 126 guns that could shoot cannon balls up to two miles. These muzzle-loading cannons were never fired in anger and soon became obsolete.

After a few periods of revival, in 1970 Fort Point was declared a **National Historic Site** and it's now part of the Golden Gate National Recreation Area (GGNRA). It's open from 10 A.M. to 5 P.M. daily (except Christmas and New Year's Day) and has a small museum. About every forty-five minutes on most weekends, rangers, many in Civil War costume, lead tours; several times a year there's a free seminar on seacoast defense history. Call 415/556-1693 for information.

An easy and scenic way to reach Fort Point is to walk the zigzag trail down from the bridge toll plaza parking area, which you can reach on Muni bus #28. Call 415/673-MUNI for Muni schedules or 415/332-6600 for Golden Gate Transit buses. Driving to Fort Point is tricky. Going north on Highway 101, take the last exit before the Toll Plaza that reads, "Presidio—Golden Gate NRA." Turn right immediately, then left onto Lincoln Boulevard, and left on Long to the end at the seawall. Going south, stay in the Golden Gate Bridge's right lane. Just after the toll plaza, take the 25th Avenue exit right, passing under the Toll Plaza and through the view area to Lincoln Boulevard, then turn left on Long.

Golden Gate Promenade to the Marina Green

East of Fort Point, looking towards San Francisco's skyline, are over three miles of probably the world's most scenic urban trail, the well-paved **Golden Gate Promenade** used by joggers, hikers, bikers, people in wheelchairs, and parents pushing strollers. Besides the view all around you, there's a small **sandy beach** for happy dogs and humans, barefoot or otherwise, here on the north border of **Crissy Field**. Eventually, if the Golden Gate National Park Association can raise enough money, this park will acquire more sandy beach, dunes and native plantings, a one-and-a-half-acre saltwater lagoon for children, and additional parking and restrooms.

Among the pleasant minisurprises along this priceless portion of the GGNRA is the stone **viewing site** off the public parking lot just west of the **Saint Francis Yacht Club**. This morsel of tranquility was dedicated to socialite Lita Vietor in

Fort Point and the Golden Gate Bridge after a storm.

1985. As you gaze out towards the Marin Headlands and Golden Gate, you can see why—as the plaque reads—"This was her favorite place."

Although the prestigious Saint Francis Yacht Club is private, you can walk—and **fish**—along the Bay's edge north of the club buildings, past the old stone **lighthouse**. This **public trail** continues by the small Golden Gate Yacht Club to the end of the jetty.

Here, within feet of where yachts and racing sailboats enter and leave the marina, you can sit on tiered stone steps to drink in the scenery and listen to the **Wave Organ** music from the Bay's waves. This public art was conceived by sculptor Peter Richards and designed "as we went along" by enthusiastic fellow sculptors, stone masons, and students. The result, depending on the tides and your imagination, can be magic. (Or it can sound like a toilet flushing.)

Marina Green West, complete with a welcome restroom, adjoins. There's also a stone snack bar by a shallow **wading lagoon** with huge yachts moored at its east end. Although this is **kite flying** country, **sunbathers** are usually draped on the arc of stone steps at the lagoon's northern edge, protected from the brisk afternoon breezes. More energetic types play volleyball nearby.

Palace of Fine Arts, Exploratorium, and More Marina Green

You can see one of the city's most admired and visited buildings, the **Palace of Fine Arts**, across Marina Boulevard. Like a half-forgotten dream, its ornate columns and rotunda rise many stories. If you've never visited this graceful anachronism, do. Bernard Maybeck, the architect who created it for the 1915 Panama-Pacific Exposition, believed that beauty should be soothing. He achieved this by combining trees, grass, sky, lagoon, and his creation into one harmonious unit, with statues of women weeping for the beauty of it all.

As time passed, the original palace, built of plaster over wood and chicken wire, lapsed into a magnificent ruin. But the San Francisco public would not let it be torn down. Starting in 1962 it was recreated in concrete from castings of the original. Now the sloping lawns are dotted with families enjoying the Palace as they watch birds flitting in the trees or ducks and waterbirds on the lagoon. Early risers might glimpse a red fox who sneaks over from the nearby Presidio to help himself to a waterfowl.

Another big reason to visit the Palace of Fine Arts is that renowned science museum, **The Exploratorium**, founded by physicist Frank Oppenheimer and located here. Call 415/563-7337 or recorded information at 415/563-3200 for times and fees. It's no wonder that children—admitted free—are there by the busload and that the Exploratorium has been imitated around the world. In this huge, barnlike building you can see, touch, hear, and explore facets of science, art, and technology. Where else can you admire a sea slug's nerve endings, blow bubbles the size of a dishpan, investigate the miracle of lasers, or explore the laws of gravity without getting hurt? And that's just a few of the 500 exhibits waiting to interact with you and your children.

More Marina Green to Fort Mason

The **Marina Green** continues on the eastern side of the yacht harbor to Gashouse Cove, with its forests of boat masts. On a sunny day, this front lawn of the city is crowded with **sunbathers, joggers, frisbee throwers, picnickers**, and city folk out to breathe sea-scented air or exercise on the **parcourse. Fishing** buffs can wet their lines off the catwalk at Gashouse Cove. **Kite flying** is very popular, and you may see George Ham, the "mayor of Marina Green," flying a multicolored kite or windsock as long as 115 feet.

Where to eat? For gourmet vegetarian fare if you don't mind a long wait to be seated, try **Greens** (415/771-6222) in Building B at Fort Mason, next stop east. Perhaps the restaurant planned for Pier 1 will be open by the time you show up. Some locals cross Marina Boulevard to the plush **Marina Safeway** for deli picnic fare. Note its 1960s tile murals by John Garth depicting harvests from the four corners of the world. While there, you may see busloads of Japanese tourists attracted by this supermarket. Drivers who bring them here enroute to scenic attractions farther on have a difficult time prying them loose from the grocery displays. Across from Safeway on

Picnickers enjoy the afternoon at the Palace of Fine Arts.

Buchanan, past the Yoga College, is **Just Desserts**, which is self-explanatory. A few blocks south, restaurants of many nationalities stretch along Lombard near Fillmore.

Fort Mason

Fort Mason is a creative and exciting way to turn swords into plowshares. From 1913 to 1962 it was a troop transport center; in World War II more than a million soldiers embarked from its docks. Since it became part of the GGNRA, the cavernous buildings and piers in the lower portion house a smorgasbord of organizations, mostly nonprofit educational, ecological, cultural, or arts-related. A **photography center** to honor Ansel Adams is planned for Pier 1.

Greenpeace, the Oceanic Society, the Magic Theatre, a Maritime Museum with historic documents, and Mexican and other ethnic museums are tenants. Drop by or write the Fort Mason Foundation, Building A, San Francisco, CA 94123 (415/441-5706) for the complete listing and a calendar of the hundreds of events, like folk festivals, that take place here. Maps and information are also on kiosks in the huge, free parking lot.

You can glimpse Alcatraz and the Bay between the many old (but repainted) buildings and can watch ships passing closeup from the piers. **Fishing** is OK off Pier 2 and on the side of Pier 3 opposite to where you can board the World War II **Liberty Ship, Jeremiah O'Brien** (415/441-3101) for a small fee. Most people fish on the wind-whipped western pier sides instead of the balmy leeward edge. Inside Pier 2 are **murals** of the Bay and its history, but the public can see them only during events held here. Near the *O'Brien*, however, you can admire an outside **mural** of grizzlies, pelicans, and other wildlife taking over a decomposing San Francisco freeway.

A bullet-shaped **Bufano statue** guards the steep steps leading up and across the Golden Gate Promenade to **Upper Fort Mason**. More sculptures, many in metal, are scattered about this quiet, grassy area where the Army still holds forth in a few mid-nineteenth century houses. A colorful surprise is the **Community Garden** where local San Franciscans tend tiny plots. The garden is fenced so you can admire, but not pick.

An elephantine wooden building is now headquarters of the Golden Gate National Recreation Area, the most visited unit of the country's National Park Service. Weekdays from 7:30 A.M. to 5 P.M. you can stop in for information; or call 415/556-0560. The **San Francisco International Hostel** (415/771-7277), part of American Youth Hostels, Inc., has ninety-six bunks in a historic Civil War barracks. The hostel insists it's for the young of heart of all ages. Paths lead down from behind the hostel to a shaded **picnic area** near the recently restored 230-foot-long brick artillery emplacement, **Black Point Battery**, a Spanish-built fort built before the Civil War to protect the Bay.

Aquatic Park

Parking at or near **Aquatic Park** can be hazardous to your blood pressure and budget. A beautiful way to get there is to hike the **Golden Gate Promenade** after you park at Fort Mason. Bring your camera and join the others who pause along this easy walk to have their pictures snapped with the gold-red bridge, Bay, and Alcatraz in the background.

As you descend to the end of the promenade, you notice a disintegrating dock. Once it served launches and transports going to and from Alcatraz. Now it's used by seagulls and a few anglers and crabbers. The building jammed against the hill to the south is a San Francisco Fire Department High Pressure Pumping Station, which assures that the city will always have water; the 1906 quake and fire haven't been forgotten.

You get an excellent overview of the 1,850-foot circular concrete **fishing** jetty, known as the **Muni Pier**, and the Hyde Street Pier and Fisherman's Wharf breakwaters that protect this sandy Aquatic Park lagoon. Some lifeguards here contend that this cove has the safest **swimming beach** in the Bay Area. Certainly all year long dauntless types in bright caps do a fast crawl through the 55 degree Fahrenheit—or less—water. Many of them belong to the Dolphin or South End clubs, founded circa 1850. Long male bastions, these private swimming and rowing clubs had to admit the public, including females, when the GGNRA took over.

Suddenly, after the quiet of the Golden Gate Promenade, you're confronted with cars nosing in for nonexistent parking, bongo drums, and the hum of civilization. The good news? You'll find restrooms, a **snack bar** that sells cold beer, and grassy beach areas, one protected from the winds. You may also meet José and Rosalie, the immigrant great-tailed grackles who have taken up residence here and panhandle French-fried potatoes at the snack bar. Besides scenery, other vistas include rows of scantily clad sunbathers on stone bleachers overlooking the cove.

For a change of pace, take a short detour to the **bocce ball courts**, off Van Ness. To find them, follow the sound of shouting, mostly in Italian, as the contestants play this ancient bowling game.

The **National Maritime Museum** (415/556-8177), built by the WPA (Work Progress Administration) in 1930's Depression days to resemble a ship's superstructure, has Art Moderne touches that include murals and terrazzo marble floors. Admission is free to gaze at anchors, bowsprits, ship models, photographs, and artifacts of a rich and varied maritime past. The building also houses shower facilities for swimmers and the nation's oldest senior center (415/775-1866).

Is there a San Francisco tourist who has not ridden a cable car? Instead of taking a Mason Street car from downtown to Fisherman's Wharf, the fortunate fight their way on to the Hyde Street cars that end up at a charming gaslit **Victorian Plaza** after plunging down Hyde towards the Bay. This plaza is alive with vivid flower plantings, musicians, benches, pigeons, and machines that vend tickets so that shivering tourists can stand in line for tickets to take a cable car back "halfway to the stars." Muni buses #19, #30, #32, and #42 also come to or close to here.

Included in this great site, and part of the GGNRA, is the **Hyde Street Pier**, with the world's largest collection of old historic ships still afloat. For no admission fee you can board a "walking beam" ferryboat, an 1895 sailing schooner, or view an 1891 scow-schooner and a 1907 oceangoing steam tug. A special program allows children to stay overnight on some of these old ships; call 415/556-6435 for information.

On weekends you can often get in on living history demonstrations, perhaps learn how to tie knots or join in singing sea chanties. Dozens of old-time seagoing items are displayed around the pier. The bookstore carries a huge selection of maritime books, many for children. And there's more. For a small fee you can board the *Balclutha*, an 1886 square-rigged Cape Horn sailing ship, anchored farther east at Pier 43; you see its three tall masts from far away.

The GGNRA is rehabilitating the historic brick **Haslett Warehouse**, at the south end of Aquatic Park. A portion of the building will serve as an exhibition annex of the National Maritime Museum. The park people hope to eventually have one of the best maritime museums in the country. They're off to a good start.

Another historic oasis in this popular area is the **Buena Vista Cafe** (415/474-5044) at the foot of Hyde Street. The B.V. calls itself probably the oldest (1889) and busiest(!) bar in San Francisco. This "clamorous and cosmopolitan" cafe serves surprisingly inexpensive lunch and dinner specials provided you find space to sit. If you manage this feat, you will be elbow to elbow with tourists, honchos from downtown, boaters, or—you name it. The B.V.'s main fame is Irish Coffee, a rich concoction of Irish whiskey, coffee, and whipped cream that must be tried, and retried, and tried again.

Young architects enjoy the sandy beach at Aquatic Park.

SAN FRANCISCO NORTH COMMERCIAL WATERFRONT & EMBARCADERO

Fisherman's Wharf Area

Can millions of tourists be wrong? They visit **Fisherman's Wharf** partly because San Francisco's most desirable cable car rides end up near there, but mostly because they want to take in the sights they've heard so much about. Purists may call this tourist Mecca trinkety, but between shops hawking T-shirts, cable car paperweights, and Alcatraz prison caps are priceless glimpses of Bay and boats, plus touches of serenity.

As for picturesqueness, you can't avoid it on a Sunday in mid-October during the **Columbus Day Parade** down Columbus Avenue. The previous Sunday is even more colorful when Sicilian matrons and Knights of Columbus straggle from St. Peter and Paul's church at Washington Square to Fisherman's Wharf for the **Blessing of the Fishing Fleet**.

What's left of the actual working waterfront is authentic. A handful of fishermen still carry on the trade of their Genoese and Sicilian forefathers who emigrated to sunny North Beach decades ago. In midafternoon a few sport fishing and commercial boats, trailed by clamoring seagulls, chug back with their catch. You can see and smell the action close-up from Fish Alley on the north side of the tiny harbor between Leavenworth and Jones, behind Fisherman's Grotto. Later on you may meet a visiting sea lion, who achieved her overly plump figure by begging for fish.

Back along Jefferson and Taylor the carnival continues: street vendors hawking art, jewelry, or other souvenirs; the Guinness Museum of World Records; street entertainers; fast-food stops; a Wax Museum, a pinball emporium, and Ripley's Believe It or Not Museum; sidewalk counters dispensing San Francisco's famous sourdough bread and walk-away seafood cocktails. But don't anticipate fresh crab; most crabs that end up in your cocktail are caught frozen or in cans. If you insist on a sit-down meal in the area, three restaurants with excellent views are Tarantino's (415/775-5600), Scoma's (415/771-4383), and the Franciscan (415/362-7733).

Public transportation to this congested area? Downtown at Powell and Market those with fortitude can board the Powell/Mason cable car to the wharf or the Powell/Hyde line, which deposits you two blocks west after an unforgettable ride. The #32 bus runs along the Embarcadero; catch it by the Ferry Building at the foot of Market Street. The #15 Kearny bus and #30 Stockton trolleybus pass the Moscone Center and cross Market on Third Street. Both travel through Chinatown and North Beach, but the crowded #30, nicknamed the Orient Express, takes forever. From the Civic Center area take the #47 Van Ness or #19 Polk buses. Call 415/673-MUNI for information. Driving? Nearby parking is expensive; it might pay to taxi from downtown.

Some olden-time Fisherman's Wharf color has faded, but at least now there are public restrooms and a few benches where you can watch marine action on the Bay. (The pier just east of Fisherman's Wharf is called Vista Pier for a reason.) You're not hallucinating if you see a submarine moored off the east side of Pier 45. It's the World War II *Pampanito*, which agile types can tour for a small fee.

From Pier 43½ the Red & White Fleet's ferries (415/546-2896) embark on Bay **harbor tours** to Tiburon or Sausalito. Some also go to Angel Island (see pages 97–100.). Whirring Commodore Helicopters land and take off on **sightseeing flights** from Pier 43, close to where the **Balclutha**, an 1886, square-rigged Cape Horn sailing ship, quietly creaks at anchor, welcoming landlubbers aboard for a small stipend. Red and White ferries for Alcatraz and Vallejo leave from Pier 41. Farther east yet, at Pier 39, the Blue & Gold Fleet (415/781-7877) also offers Bay cruises.

Fisherman's Wharf isn't the only location crammed with shops. Near the cable car turnaround at Taylor and Bay is **Cost Plus Imports**, with a gigantic selection of gifts and gadgets from around the globe. Outside, lines of street vendors sell art, artifacts, and, of course, T-shirts. Near Beach and Taylor streets **Benny Bufano's statue of St. Francis** blesses the passing throngs from the I.L.W.U. (International Longshoreman's and Warehouseman's Union) parking lot. The late sculptor, a small man, has a big following in the Bay Area.

Hyde Street cable car plunging to the Bay's shore.

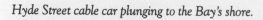

Ghirardelli Square, The Cannery, and Anchorage

Perhaps the most noted shopping and dining complex within walking distance of Fisherman's Wharf is **Ghirardelli** (pronounced GEAR-ar-deli) **Square**, a two-and-a-half-acre award-winning landmark across from Aquatic Park between Beach, Polk, Larkin, and North Point streets. Browsers enjoy eight levels of views and landscaping in fourteen red brick buildings that once housed a woolen mill and chocolate factory. Sculptor Ruth Asawa's fountain with a mermaid and other playful creatures, is the hub. Appropriately, it's on Fountain Plaza. The Information Booth (415/775-5500) at 900 North Point, also on Fountain Plaza, hands out free maps and lists of the eighty or so tenants: galleries for fine art to folk art, jewelry and craft shops, plus fashion boutiques.

Where to eat and park? Many restaurants are ethnic; almost all have superb views. Two well-known restaurants are four-star: Maxwell's Plum (415/441-4140) and The Mandarin (415/673-8812). Wallet undernourished? You can buy popcorn, Ghirardelli chocolate, or bagels from pushcarts. Underground **parking** off Beach is not inexpensive, but many Ghirardelli establishments offer free validation.

After the success of Ghirardelli Square, **The Cannery**, at 2801 Leavenworth (415/771-3112) resurrected itself from a 1909 peach-canning plant. It contains about fifty shops, restaurants, and galleries. Views, especially from the third floor, are recommended, and musicians and entertainers perform in the sunken Cannery Courtyard on the lower level. (Tip to visitors from colder climes: Don't eat olives that drop from the ancient trees here; they're bitter until they've been treated.)

The Anchorage (415/775-6000), east of the Cannery between Beach and Jefferson, is a comparative newcomer. It advertises that its restaurants and shops have an international tang.

Pier 39

About two blocks east of Fisherman's Wharf at the foot of Stockton Street, you see the gray bulk of **Pier 39**. This forty-five-acre pier located between two marinas offers dining, shopping, and entertainment, not to mention the waterfront views; the pier juts out into the Bay to give you a look at The City, too. Pier 39 was built of actual and fake weathered timbers with walkways all around and benches. Colorful flowers and plants have been carefully selected to thrive in this breezy, salt-seasoned air.

A double-deck **carousel** is popular with kids and a Funtasia Entertainment Center has rides, video games, and games of skill. Jugglers, mimes, and musicians perform outside. As for indoor entertainment, at the San Francisco Experience Theatre you're involved with the sights, sounds, and sensations of San Francisco, past and present. The **shops?** Many of the hundred or so are specialized. Ready Teddy, the Left Hand World, Magnet P.I., and Kitemakers of San Francisco are self-explanatory. There are, of course, boutiques, galleries, jewelery and craft shops, and—yes—a few that sell T-shirts.

Where to eat on Pier 39? You'll find plenty of fast fare. Two sit-down seafood restaurants for lunch and dinner are Dante's Sea Catch (415/421-5778) and Chic's

Place (415/421-2442). For breakfast and lunch only, the casual **Eagle Cafe** (415/433-3689) is beloved by locals: fishermen, cab drivers, nearby workers, plus arty and professional types from downtown. Although it now roosts on the second floor of Pier 39, this cafe started life a few blocks away in 1928. When it was about to be demolished in the name of urban renewal, the cry of anguish was so loud the actual cafe was moved over the Embarcadero and lifted up by crane. The Eagle's cafeteria food is hearty and inexpensive, and the bar dispenses t.l.c. long after lunch ends at two P.M.

A walkway from Pier 39 over the Embarcadero leads to a **parking** garage that holds 1,000 vehicles. Like other paid parking in the area, it's expensive. Some Pier 39 restaurants offer free validation, but only after 6 P.M.

The Embarcadero North

Minutes after you walk east on the Embarcadero from thronged Fisherman's Wharf and Pier 39, you'll experience relative calm, starting at small, grassy Sidney Rudy **Waterfront Park.** It overlooks a marina with many yachts and an occasional tall ship. Besides benches and a small **parcourse** for exercising, the park features a soaring silver "Skygate" sculpture by Peter Barr dedicated to the late Eric Hoffer, "longshoreman, poet, philosopher."

Pier 35, next, is an actual passenger terminal where you might see a huge liner arrive or depart in a rainbow of confetti; check San Francisco's big daily newspapers for listings. Note: Uneven-numbered piers 1 to 45 are north of the Ferry Building; even-numbered piers 24 to 98 are south. Note 2: There's two-hour metered parking along stretches of the Embarcadero; any car overstaying its welcome quickly acquires a parking ticket.

Where to eat? Many San Franciscans come to the north Embarcadero to dine as they absorb the waterfront ambience. One popular spot for breakfast and lunch or a drink—since the bar has the best view—is the Peer Inn (415/788-1453) at Pier 33. Next east, also on Pier 33, is the City Yacht Club Restaurant (415/788-4814) which admits yachtsmen and nonyacht owners for lunch, dinner, and Sunday brunch. It also has a Bay view plus a small parking area between Pier 33 and 31. Anchored nearby are Hornblower Party Yachts (415/434-0300); they give Bay lunch cruises on Friday and dinner cruises most days.

Across the Embarcadero—and crossing on foot is a challenge—is a path through a small landscaped office park. Farther south is the neon-lit Fog City Diner (415/982-2000), a trendy new-wave restaurant at 1300 Battery. If the new wave hasn't ebbed by the time you arrive, you can try its extensive lunch and dinner menu which lists "unintimidating mixed greens."

Levi's Plaza and Telegraph Hill

Just inland from the Embarcadero on Battery is **Levi's Plaza,** six blocks of green open space where downtowners, out-of-towners, and employees of the adjoining Levi Strauss corporate headquarters can loll and stroll. A sparkling stream, edged with granite blocks and benches, courses through this creative mix of rolling hills and trees. The courtyard features a cascading fountain you can walk around or through, to the delight of children. A few blocks away concrete skyscrapers loom, but at Levi's Plaza the buildings are brick and the pace is relaxed. The same goes for the small shops, like Minerva's Owl Bookstore, on the Arcade.

Where to eat? Samantha's (415/986-0100) is open weekdays for lunch and Monday through Saturday for dinner. The Il Fornaio Bakery and Cafe (415/391-4622), on the corner of Greenwich and Sansome streets, just below Telegraph Hill, is open all day weekdays and Saturday. You can join the regulars—many from the hill—inside or outside on the patio as you sip cappuccino or munch delicacies like fresh bread, croissants, or pasta. Muni bus #42 goes by, and the #32 bus that runs along the Embarcadero is close. If you drive, there's a public parking garage at Greenwich and Sansome.

Side Excursion up Telegraph Hill

For a beautiful, bucolic walk up through hillside gardens to a fragment of old San Francisco, take the steep **Filbert Street steps** that start at the north edge of the Telegraph Landing housing development west of the Levi's Plaza Fountain. It helps to have strong legs and wind, but you can rest en route.

On the way up, a plaque on a bench quotes Dorothy in the Land of Oz: "I have a

A feline resident of Telegraph Hill admires paintings on the Filbert Steps.

feeling we're not in Kansas any more." True. Kansas never had views like this—back towards the Bay Bridge and Treasure Island—from shadowed hillside lanes. Napier Lane is particularly charming. Artists still set up easels to paint the tiny, many-hued, pre-1906 earthquake homes and flowers along this tilting wooden lane, where neighbors stop to chat or exchange messages on an outside blackboard.

The **Grace Marchant Garden** is a highlight, especially when you realize its late creator spent thirty-three years of her own time and money transforming debris-ridden east Filbert Street, too steep for cars, into this profusion of plants and trees: roses and baby tears, palms and sequoias. When Grace became frail, Gary Kray and fellow neighbors helped out. Since her death, Kray has continued caring for the garden, now saved for the public by the efforts of F.O.G. (Friends of the Garden). On the walk you can pause to watch an arresting array of felines pounce on butterflies, as wind chimes tinkle and doves, finches, escaped tropical birds, and other winged wildlife fly about.

Then from Montgomery Street at the top of the steps you can zig north to Greenwich and up brick steps to the 274-foot crest of **Telegraph Hill** with its 210-foot high **Coit Tower** probing the skyline. If you're not in the mood for a strenuous walk up Telegraph Hill, Muni bus #39 goes to Coit Tower from the Fisherman's Wharf area or from Washington Square in North Beach. Try to avoid driving; there's limited space at the top. However you get there, take enough film for your camera.

Back to the Embarcadero North

If it continued on to the Embarcadero, a direct line from Filbert Street would end at **Pier 23,** the foreign trade zone. Attached to the pier's side is the small Pier 23 Cafe (415/362-5125) with a view towards Treasure Island from its white linen-covered tables and miniscule deck. Lunch and dinner are served weekdays and brunch on Sunday, but Pier 23 is most famous for Dixieland jazz. Wednesday through Saturday nights and Sunday from 4 to 9, devotees from myriad lands and social circles gather. Herb Caen, the city's reigning columnist, might even squeeze in.

San Francisco's North Embarcadero has changed since Harry Bridges and the longshoreman's union were headline material. Along this stretch, the briefcase has replaced the longshoreman's hook, and architects, lawyers, and advertising people occupy many piers and old ferry boats, like the *Klamath* at Pier 5, taken over by Landor Associates.

Pier 7 is open for free fishing all week and for paid parking, with a bargain rate from 11:30 to 6 weekdays. Plans call for a new parklike Pier 7, which will be welcome. Also at Pier 7, the Waterfront Restaurant (415/391-2696) dispenses lunch, dinner, and Sunday brunch. You can see water from several levels; the small outside deck is within splashing distance of working pilot boats. For simple, inexpensive food in a hurry, try Pier 1 just north of the Ferry Building. The napkins are paper, but there's a restroom.

Justin Herman Plaza

On weekdays, especially when it's sunny, **Justin Herman Plaza,** across the Embarcadero, is filled with strollers, outdoor street artists, picnickers, and people relaxing at outdoor cafes, along with pigeons that flutter onto the tables. To the east the overhead Embarcadero Freeway curves towards the San Francisco–Oakland Bay Bridge, hiding most of the landmark Ferry Building.

To the west the gigantic concrete slabs of the Embarcadero Center's four office buildings rise above three levels of open plazas and over 175 shops and restaurants. Many are connected by promenades above the street, but that's another story. Do view the soaring seventeen-story Atrium of the Hyatt Hotel, just off the plaza at Market Street. Besides, on Friday there's free tea dancing in the lobby from 5:30 to 8:30 P.M.

A modern stainless steel sculpture decorates the Market Street side of Justin Herman Plaza, but you're more aware of the **Vaillancourt Fountain's** great jets of water splashing through a jumble of square tubing. The fact that it's controversial doesn't bother the admiring bystanders or the adventurous adults and children who walk through its watery concrete maze. A small **parcourse** for exercise buffs hides behind the fountain, but relaxing is the main occupation on the plaza, and there are plenty of benches, steps, and plots of grass where you can do it. As a bonus, near the gazebo on summer Sundays, starting at 1 P.M., there's a free jazz concert.

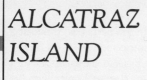

ALCATRAZ ISLAND

Doing Time on the Rock

Once underworld characters like Al Capone, "Machine Gun" Kelly, and famous birdman Robert Stroud were its reluctant guests. Now **Alcatraz Island** is in the Golden Gate National Recreation Area, and every day, except Thanksgiving, Christmas, and New Year's Day, boatloads of eager visitors—more than half a million a year—take a ferry from San Francisco to do time on The Rock.

Even before it became a prison for incorrigible criminals, Alcatraz had a rocky history. In 1775 its discoverer, Spanish explorer Juan Manuel de Ayala, saw only twelve barren acres of fog-draped rock with no vegetation, merely a layer of guano indicating that the island was popular with birds. The Spanish name *Alcatraces* was meant for Yerba Buena Island; a cartographer goofed and the name stuck. Evidently historic sources goofed, too. According to the official GGNRA historian, *Alcatraces* refers to cormorants, not pelicans, as is commonly believed.

In 1853, to help protect the Bay, Alcatraz became a fort and the Army added batteries and fortifications and carved brick-walled magazines (not dungeons) into the rock. In 1854 the West Coast's first U.S. lighthouse was built; day and night its 214-foot successor, erected in 1909, beams light twenty-one miles out to sea.

Alcatraz started being used as a prison in 1861. Between then and 1933, the military jailed Civil War deserters, renegade Indians, and soldiers convicted of various offenses. Alcatraz also acted as a temporary San Francisco jail after the 1906 quake and fire. Then in 1934 sealed trains, containing prisoners, were barged over and Alcatraz became a federal penitentiary for more than 1,500 of the toughest convicts in the United States. As time went by, Alcatraz achieved its unsavory, spine-chilling reputation.

When the penitentiary was closed in 1963 because of deteriorating facilities, public opposition, and expense (it cost $30,000 to keep one prisoner one year), no one could decide what to do with the deserted rock. Should it be returned to the cormorants and pelicans, become the pedestal for an enormous sculpture for peace, or what? In the hiatus, groups of native Americans from many tribes moved over, claiming the surplus land as rightfully theirs. During their nineteen-month occupation, a fire damaged the lighthouse and several buildings. In 1971 the few remaining protestors were removed without incident. "Indian Land" was no more.

Most movies about Alcatraz depict its clanking doors, riots, and escapes. Seeing this Devil's Island of America in person, you understand why Robert Kennedy called it a place of horror. A prisoner lived in a cell five by eight by seven-and-a-half feet high, furnished with a cot, toilet, wash basin, and shelf. Isolation was broken only for three twenty-minute meals and rare exercise periods. Conversation was forbidden. A prisoner who obeyed all rules could see his lawyer or a family member for one hour per month, with guards listening. No wonder some prisoners were driven mad.

The full horror strikes you when you visit the "hole," reserved for the more violent cases. On occasion the inmate sent here might spend his nights and days in utter darkness, with only a hole in the floor for sanitary purposes. Rangers now ask for volunteers to step inside. When the steel door clangs shut and the darkness grows darker, the temporary inmates can stand it for only a few minutes.

Alcatraz, resembling a gray battleship, is anchored a mere mile away from The City. Yet the Bay's chilling water and swirling tides, to say nothing of one guard to each ten convicts, kept escapes down. At least thirty-nine prisoners tried; perhaps five made it. In 1937 two men went over the fence and disappeared into thick fog. Rumors persist that they were seen later, alive and comfortable, in South America. The rest drowned, were shot to death, or were recaptured. One escapee who swam the distance was washed ashore, half dead, and "rescued" by police. Rangers joke that they scrutinize visitors' faces to be sure a successful escapee isn't returning. Actually, there are nostalgic returnees: the families who lived here during the prison period;

Sealed trains deposited incorrigible prisoners on Alcatraz starting in 1934.

their children were ferried to school in San Francisco. They remember Alcatraz as a small friendly village.

At first, after it became a park, visitors had to stay in groups, guided by rangers the minute they stepped off the ferry. Now, after a suggested slide show, you can buy an inexpensive brochure for a self-guided tour. Along the way, especially inside the musty cell block, rangers present programs. On your own, you can enjoy many facets of this island with its 360-degree views of Bay, city, and passing ships.

Then there are the **birds**—perhaps strings of geese flying over, necks stretched out. Noisy black-crowned night herons bring up their offspring in trees near the path leading up from the dock. Western gulls nest all over the island, often so close to paths you easily see their fluffy gray chicks. Many other birds visit or use the air space.

For a once soil-less island, the number of plants is surprising. The **Gardens of Alcatraz** started when dirt from nearby Angel Island was brought over to form battery emplacements. As Alcatraz became a more settled military post and homes were built, formal gardens flourished. Now thirty varieties of trees and plants, even roses, survive only on the moisture from fog and rain.

To do your time on The Rock, don comfortable shoes and a warm sweater and head for the Red & White Fleet's Pier 41 ticket office (415/546-2805) at the foot of Powell Street near Fisherman's Wharf. If you show up before 8 A.M., you might get tickets for that day. In winter ferries leave hourly until early afternoon; in summer (Memorial Day to Labor Day) the schedule is increased.

Food? You can bring your lunch and picnic in the balmy area near the dock. The boat has snack bars, but they sell cold beer only on the return trip to San Francisco. What happens if you miss the last boat back? You are cited and given the privilege of taking a water taxi. The cost? $200.00 plus citation.

SAN FRANCISCO WATERFRONT FROM THE FERRY BUILDING SOUTH

The Ferry Building

The matronly, graying 1896 Ferry Building still reigns at the foot of Market Street. But skyscrapers, the Embarcadero Freeway, and the San Francisco–Oakland Bay Bridge partially block views of her 240-foot tower, cupola, and four-faced clock that stopped at 5:16 A.M., April 18, 1906. It took a year to repair the quake-damaged clocks, but they've been chiming the hours ever since. There's talk of renovating the old landmark, but two long-term tenants are reluctant to give up their leases, so the project is on hold. At present the World Trade Center occupies most of the north wing. The most important point of interest there may be the small public restroom, scarce in these parts, off the street hallway.

Before the era of bridges, the Ferry Building was the main portal through which up to 100,000 ferry riders descended on the city daily. Now they arrive in cars and buses or under the Bay on **BART** (Bay Area Rapid Transit). (In fact, BART's transbay tube passes under the Ferry Building on its way to the nearby Embarcadero Station.) But **Golden Gate Ferries** still run to Sausalito and Larkspur from a terminal built on the platform around the BART ventilator; ferries to Tiburon use a short dock north of the Ferry Building during commute hours. The city has provided benches so you can wait for or watch the ferries in comfort. But why not take a ferry ride yourself? Call 415/332-6600 for times and fees.

Fishing hopefuls and **crabbers** try their luck on a pedestrian mall near the BART ventilation shaft. Views from here are out towards Treasure Island and back towards San Francisco. The panorama is even better from the second floor of The Ferry Plaza Restaurant (415/391-8403). At Sinbad's (415/781-2555), just south on Pier 2, you can lunch outside on a deck open to public access. In a hurry? At a brightly painted cart in front of the Ferry Building you can buy hot dogs, snacks, and lottery tickets.

A landscaped, concrete **Marine Promenade** replaced several decayed piers south of the Ferry Building. Now you can join strollers, joggers, brown baggers, and Bay watchers who like comparatively fresh air. This ia a far cry from the days when longshoremen swaggered along the waterfront. A memorial to those times is the depression-type **mural-sculpture** depicting the bloody 1934 San Francisco water-front strike. It's at Mission and Steuart streets on the south edge of the grassy Embarcadero park, where traditional statues of Juan Bautista de Anza and Spanish king Carlos III, who helped found San Francisco, gaze out at locals and visitors napping on the turf.

The **Fireboat Dock**, near Pier 24 in the shadow of the San Francisco–Oakland Bay Bridge, seems small. It will look even smaller when highrise South Beach waterfront developments, from the bridge to near China Basin, are finished. A wide boulevard will front the Bay and new 700-berth marina. Plans call for a four-and-a-half-acre waterfront park, housing, and, hopefully, a Muni light vehicle rail line from Market Street to China Basin. The present maze of Belt Line Rail tracks will be reduced to one. Hills Brothers Coffee employees will remain in their brick building, but the coffee refinery itself, along with the zesty aroma that welcomed Bay commuters for so many years, has already moved to the foot of Potrero Hill.

San Francisco–Oakland Bay Bridge and Treasure Island

San Francisco's Golden Gate Bridge is on more postcards than the silvery **San Francisco–Oakland Bay Bridge**, which opened in November 1936. But this less-photographed span is busier and longer, carrying Interstate-80 over almost four miles of Bay. It has its own beauty: Egrets station themselves at intervals along the East Bay shoreline approach, and the panorama from the top deck as you start your

The ferry to Sausalito and Larkspur takes off from the Market Street Ferry Building.

descent into San Francisco is worth a thousand words, especially during the frequent traffic tie-ups.

About half way across, a tunnel burrows through **Yerba Buena Island**, presently under the jurisdiction of the Navy. Originally Indians fished there. Then it became a goat farm, acquiring the name Goat Island. In the 1870s the Lighthouse Service built a fog signal and pristine white lighthouse, which is still in use. Around the turn of the century, the Navy opened a training center, prompting the historic comment that the island went from "goats to greenhorns."

Most of Yerba Buena Island and **Treasure Island** are off limits, except for the free Navy–Marine–Coast Guard **Museum** (415/765-6182), open 10:00 A.M. to 3:30 P.M. daily except holidays. This art deco building was part of the grandiose 1939–1940 Golden Gate International Exposition. In fact, Treasure Island itself was built for the event on 400 acres of shoals. The museum shows nostalgic photographs and posters of the fair period, plus uniforms and capsule histories of United States military encounters. One exhibit describes the World War II Navajo code talkers, Indians who delivered messages in the Navajo language that the enemy was unable to decipher.

Turnoffs to Treasure Island are on either side of the tunnel. On a clear day or night, drive off and park on the edge facing San Francisco. This may be the Bay's best vantage point to view the skyline of The City known as Bagdad by the Bay (thanks to Herb Caen).

South Waterfront Eateries and Points of Interest

Fat Ron's and similar waterfront hangouts along the South Embarcadero are being replaced by fancy office buildings with sculptures and fountains. The Embarcadero Y.M.C.A. (415/392-2191) still offers inexpensive accommodations for men and women. Tiny, almost-too-authentic Carmen's remains at Pier 24. The more sophisticated Boondocks (415/777-1588), with its sliver of view off Pier 28, still serves lunch Monday through Friday and brunch on Saturday.

Red's Java House (415/788-9747) at the foot of Pier 30 is a genuine old-time cafe with modest prices for snacks, double cheeseburgers, and such. Historic maritime photographs and mottos crowd the wall. A typical one is: "When all is said and done, more will be said than done." Tom and Mike McGarvey, who grew up "within smelling distance of the waterfront" have run the cafe for three decades. Once it was a haven for longshoremen, teamsters, and reporters. A few fishermen, construction workers, and sailors (when the big Navy ships are moored nearby) eat breakfast or lunch, drink beer, or play the pinball machine, but office workers make up the biggest percentage of customers now.

When the 700-berth marina, office buildings, and a new restaurant are finished, the funky Java House on Pier 40 may have departed. However, the three-masted Dolphin P. Rempp shipboard restaurant (415/777-5771) is still parked high on land at Pier 42. The schooner was built in 1908 in Denmark for the lumber trade and carried supplies in World Wars I and II. Now Tuesday through Saturday at 5:00 P.M. you're welcomed aboard for cocktails. When the ship bell rings at 6:00, you can move up to the next deck for dinner.

The Dolphin restaurant is elegant. The Bouncer's Cafe, an old-time bistro inland at 66 Townsend, does not pretend to be. The walls and ceiling are layered with reminders of the waterfront's brawling past, and stevedores and other working types line the long bar. Bouncer's offers food, including a low-priced daily special, along with the funky atmosphere.

Continuing south, the docks, terminals, and industrial buildings are interrupted by **Mission Creek**, alias **China Basin**, named for the Pacific Mail Steamship lines that once discharged passengers from China here. Before the Mission Creek Development, envisioned by railroad interests, surrounds the tiny marina and houseboat community, turn inland on Berry Street to check out this alternate way of life in the shadow of the Highway 280 freeway.

But first you pass the gigantic blue China Basin Building, which now houses upscale offices. Weekdays from 7 A.M. to 5 P.M. you can treat yourself to budget-priced food at the Wharfside Hofbrau (415/495-6375). Unless you encounter a monsoon, eat outside on the deck overlooking the channel. The few boats you'll watch coming and going include the *Ruby*, a 64-foot sloop (415/861-2165) that makes luncheon charter boat jaunts around Alcatraz, and other **Bay boat excursions**.

You may also see one of the two drawbridges over China Basin creek open. The bulky **Third Street drawbridge**, in operation since 1933, is more famous than the Fourth Street drawbridge, built in 1917. It's bigger, and its trunion bascule lift was designed by Joseph B. Strauss, engineer for the Golden Gate Bridge.

Across Fourth Street in an unprepossessing wooden building on an old pier decorated with a few trees in containers is Blanche's (415/397-4191), a San Francisco institution for more than two decades. Weekdays from 11 A.M. to midafternoon, devotees line up to partake of shrimp sandwiches or salad plus wine in plastic glasses. Since Blanche's possesses few inside tables, the lure must be the deck that overlooks the Mission Creek houseboat community.

During early Spanish and Mexican eras, boats could travel all the way from the Bay to Mission Dolores. Around 1850 industrial fill began to invade Mission Creek. Now only a few dozen boats and wildly assorted houseboats rise and fall in what's left of the tidal waterway. Their owners, banded together in the **Mission Creek Conservancy** to protect their placid way of life, are proud that herons and showy egrets are fellow tenants, and that fish and sea lions drop by. Along the grass-edged inlet ducks and geese, looking like garden ornaments, come to life and waddle up when a human starts to quack. If you wish to visit this informal neighborhood, you can usually park on Channel Street at the creek's southern edge.

Continuing south, Mission Creek and one-way streets complicate getting to the Bay's edge. To reach the next waterfront shrine, the **Mission Rock Resort** (415/621-5538), drive southwest on Fourth Street, turn Bayward on short Mission Rock, then right on China Basin Street. The resort is at the south edge of **Aqua Vista Park**, which has grass, benches, and a public **fishing pier**.

This famous eatery and watering hole attracts a potpourri of people: windsurfers, fishing addicts, businessmen, and boaters (who may use the guest dock). A downstairs counter dispenses hamburgers, hot dogs, and beer daily from 6:30 A.M. to whenever the bartender tires. You can enjoy this fare outside on a deck or climb to the upstairs restaurant to eat your way through a more extended menu from 8:00 A.M. to midafternoon. Try to squeeze in to the outside deck up here where you might achieve a suntan. The deck overlooks the Bethlehem shipyards and various boats and birds. Inside, the clientele plays the old-fashioned jukebox or shakes for drinks at the tiny bar. On Sunday, brunch is served.

At the end of Twenty-fourth Street off Third, a small weed- and debris-ornamented park, **Warm Water Cove**, run (or neglected) by The City, features a tiny wooden **fishing pier**. Visitors are protected from Bay breezes, and fishing can be lucky when perch, flounder, and striped bass swim in to enjoy the fish food that may flourish in the warm water discharged by the pre-earthquake steam plant in the cove.

Two even tinier parks are on the east side of the **Islais Creek** channel near the Third Street drawbridge. Fishing can be too exciting in this unlikely area. In 1958 a youth drowned near Pier 92 when a huge fish—probably a shark—pulled him and his fishing line in. If there's not enough doing, keep going. Besides fishing, you can picnic, birdwatch, windsurf, and much more at a large, new recreation area on the southern boundary of San Francisco.

Candlestick Point State Recreation Area

California's first urban state park is actually two parks. The first Candlestick Park, visible from Highway 101, takes in the big stadium where the San Francisco Giants labor with bats and the 49ers with footballs. The second park, virtually unknown, is the **Candlestick Point State Recreation Area** that has been transformed from an old garbage dump into a peaceful oasis of grass, trees, and miles of **shoreline paths** plus two **fishing piers**.

Yes, both Candlestick Parks are often windy. Stiff breezes whistle through the pass, called Alemany Gap, in the San Bruno Mountain. But most benches and picnic facilities are protected by windbreaks, and **windsurfers**, **sailboaters**, **and kite flyers** take advantage of the wind. Among the many educational activities like bird walks and fishing programs, special events include Kite and Wind Festivals.

Windy or not—and it's not always—Candlestick Park is a **birdwatching** delight. Songbirds flit about in the youthful trees. Red-tailed hawks, kestrels, and brown pelicans soar overhead. Egrets, black-crowned night herons, and other shorebirds probe the edges of that **three-and-a-half mile shoreline**. Fishing can be good, too. In spring when the herring run, sturgeons weighing up to 200 pounds have been landed off the new concrete pier.

Of the 170 acres earmarked for this urban park, 37 acres have already been developed, and 15 acres are in the process. Plans call for more picnic and grassy areas, plus **boat launching** facilities, although car-top boats can be eased into the Bay from the beach now. The park also wants a performing arts and ethnic cultural center near the Visitor Center. This small building, which presently contains a tiny aquarium and educational displays, is at 1150 Carroll Avenue off Third. From the fenced-in grassy park area, drive north around the stadium to Fitch, turn right and then left when you see a building with brightly painted murals. Call 415/557-4127 for information on special activities.

SOUTH
BAY
SHORELINE
ON THE
BAY'S
WESTERN
EDGE

San Mateo County Shoreline

South of the Candlestick Point State Recreation Area, for one-and-a-half miles, Highway 101 hugs a ribbon of shoreline in **San Mateo County** where scattered trees survive and a handful of ducks and seabirds ride the choppy waves. You can join the few people trying their luck fishing. But there are no public facilities, no added niceties. Perhaps, when you next travel this route, the hoped-for hiking and biking trail will be in. If not, there's plenty of outdoor recreation ahead, especially for **hikers, bicyclists, boaters**, and **birders**.

Brisbane Marina

If you like boating, boat watching, or just a breath of the outdoors, take the **Sierra Point** turnoff off Highway 101. Behind spanking new buildings (one looks like a huge, white Cuisinart) is one of the newest and largest small craft harbors on San Francisco Bay, the 573-berth **Brisbane Marina**. A grassy **park** with benches and picnic tables and a **trail** winds around the shoreline by a small public **fishing pier** with a distant view of San Francisco.

Oyster Point and Point San Bruno

The breezy **Oyster Point and Oyster Cove** marinas at the end of the Oyster Point Boulevard turnoff in South San Francisco have a fringe of the beach-park access and a dazzling new—but short—fishing pier where, if you aren't blown away first, you might catch bullheads or smelt. You know it's near the airport because planes roar over so low all conversation must stop. Signs announce a **public path** towards **San Bruno Point** to the south, but you must walk through weeds and cross a tiny, jerry-built bridge to get there. Besides, several industries have fences right to the Bay's edge.

A nonbreezy surprise is the tiny **swimming beach** in a protected cove just north of the Oyster Point Small Boat Harbor. Since the road is blocked, you must walk over from the marina or drive again to Oyster Point Boulevard and turn right immediately after the first gray office building. Sorry, there's only the pink latrine back at the marina, but there is a shower, sunshine (usually), and a pleasant assortment of regulars, some with deep tans.

Yes, there were once oysters galore at Oyster Point. The Miwok Indians gorged on them, as you can deduce by crushed shells along the shoreline. In the late 1800s there was an oyster company nearby. Will they come back? Don't send out invitations to an oyster feed yet.

At **Point San Bruno** the outlook is superb, and planes roar over dramatically close. There are **picnic tables** and you can work out on a small **parcourse** in air that's almost too fresh. To reach this scenic but windy outlook, take the Grand Avenue exit off Highway 101 to the end.

On a hilltop overlooking it all is a gigantic **sculpture** resembling a squashed Bay Bridge that sings (or moans?) in the wind. It's on off limits California Water Company property near the top of a narrow one-lane road on Grandview, off Forbes.

Millbrae and Burlingame Bay Access

Imagine watching planes from all over the world whine to a stop several dozen yards away, as gulls and egrets forage between you and the runway! You can watch this double feature at the small **San Francisco International Airport Viewing Area** in Millbrae. People picking up passengers often relax here until they see "their" plane land. To share the excitement, take the Millbrae exit off Highway 101, turn north on Old Bayshore Highway, and follow the orange arrows on the pavement.

In **Burlingame** as you drive south on Old Bayshore, alias Airport Boulevard, you can share hidden access points with **shorebirds** behind almost every industrial building or restaurant from the Vagabond to Charlie Brown's. There's also access behind Benihana of Tokyo (415/342-5202); the Fisherman Restaurant (415/697-1490) overlooks a tiny **shorebird sanctuary** (TIP: Try the petrale as you watch the birds here). Farther south you can meander through grassy **Bayside Park** and investigate the attractive **Anza Park Lagoon** and the larger **Burlingame Lagoon**.

Kee Joon's penthouse restaurant, 433 Airport Boulevard (415/348-1122), is known for its high-level South Bay views and fine Chinese food from many provinces. You can also board a ship that never leaves shore for lunch or dinner: Near the entrance to Beach Road at 410 Airport Boulevard, the 539-ton steel-hulled ex-Bay ferry, the SS *General Frank M. Coxe*, lives out its retirement as the Pattaya Princess (415/342-9800), serving Thai or American food.

Small **Fisherman's Park** is at an L-shaped turn just south. Besides fishing off shore, habitues park and picnic as they watch airliners start their descent over forested Coyote Point.

Coyote Point County Park and on South

Coyote Point County Park was once an island surrounded by salt marsh. Now it's a peninsula, partly in Burlingame and partly in San Mateo City. It's a beautiful park. Come to just look or come to enjoy its many brands of recreation. Perhaps most appreciated is its natural **swimming beach** with lifeguards in the summer. You'll find a **child's playground, rifle range, large marina, picnic areas, and biking and**

hiking trails, in addition to the beach. Is the water safe? At Coyote Point it's checked four times a week; also, pile worms and clams are back—which may indicate the Bay is becoming less of a toxic garbage dump.

The **Coyote Point Museum** (415/342-7755), almost hidden in eucalyptus trees, is a modern institution that stresses the connection between nature and us. Huge photographs of wildlife and a replica of a whale hang from the ceiling; there are visual aids, games, live insect colonies, and other exhibits.

Down the hill (follow the sound of excited children) is the old-fashioned **Animal Center** (415/573-2600) where you can gaze at stuffed animals and birds, stroke a live gopher snake, touch a screech owl's feathers, or stand five feet away from a caged coyote. (No, the park was not named for coyotes, but probably after Coyetana Arenas who held title under an early Mexican land grant.)

If you prefer another variety of recreation, Coyote Point Park adjoins the San Mateo **Municipal Golf Course** (415/347-1461). The Castaway Restaurant (415/-347-1027) is on the grounds, overlooking the Bay and airport.

The **Shoreline Park levee trail** for pedestrians and bicyclists south of Coyote Point passes Harbor View and, later, **Ryder Court Park** on Third Avenue. Both parks are tiny but offer surcease from concrete; Ryder does boast one picnic table. **Tidelands Park**, south of a small bridge also on East Third, faces on **Marina Lagoon**, which wanders inland towards Highway 101. This undeveloped park—but perhaps that's in its favor—will be part of a much larger shoreline park after the resident dump closes. Soon that **hiking and biking trail** from Coyote Point will go all the way to Foster City's southeast edge.

If you have been yearning for a warm **sandy wading and swimming beach**, two

Parkside Aquatic Park's sandy swimming beach is usually sunny.

parks on Marina Lagoon in San Mateo City fit the bill. Delightful **Parkside Aquatic Park** on Roberta Drive also has a **boat launch** and a wagon that sells hot dogs and soft drinks. **Lakeshore Park** (Slough-side park?) farther south has a **wading beach**, but it's geared more for weekday activities. To reach either park, watch for signs on Norfolk, a through street between Highway 92 and East Third.

You can't avoid a long hike if you try the **San Mateo Fishing Pier**, in the shadow of the San Mateo Bridge. Resurrected from part of the old San Mateo–Hayward drawbridge, it juts out 4,135 feet from Foster City's edge to the South Bay's main ship channel. That long walk out and back is worth it if you bring in a big sturgeon, striped bass, or halibut. Luckily, at last report the restrooms out on the pier were again working.

Foster City and Its Lagoons and Parks

Foster City is noted for its parks and lagoons. But recently it discovered (apologies to Gertrude Stein) that the town had no "there, there." Now, twenty-six years after Jack Foster established the town on filled and diked land around the late Brewer Island, this carefully managed mix of homes and condominiums on man-made lagoons is building a downtown.

Life for Foster City's 25,000 or so residents has evolved around its ten churches, dozen or so restaurants, five small shopping centers, and those curving lagoons with their pleasant walkways and dozing ducks. But this quiet lifestyle may change when the Metro Center's twenty-two-story office building, hotels, and gigantic shopping center are finished.

At present, Foster City is a pleasant place to unwind and watch **windsurfers**

Leo J. Ryan Park in Foster City is a favorite gathering place for windsurfers.

launch their colorful craft at easy-to-reach **Leo J. Ryan Park** on Shell Boulevard, just off East Hillsdale Boulevard. From six to ten on Tuesday, April through October, as many as fifty graceful windsurfers gather to race. The park also attracts **joggers, picnickers, and sunbathers** who drape themselves on terraces overlooking the placid lagoon.

Foster City's many other parks vary from mere dots and slivers on up. **Boat Park** with its **launching dock** is just east of Leo J. Ryan Park. Erckenbrack Park, farther along, and Marlin and Gull parks across the lagoon, are easier to reach on foot than car. If strolling along walkways practically in someone's front room makes you uncomfortable, try the Pedway **walking/jogging/biking path** that parallels Beach Park Boulevard from the San Mateo Bridge to Gateshead Court off Baffin Street. The emphasis of large **Sea Cloud Park** on Belmont Slough is on **baseball**; in fact, this area may be the Little League capital of the world. To reach it, take Edgewater Drive and go right on Pitcairn Drive to the end.

Where to eat? Restaurants that overlook the lagoons include O'Donegan's (415/570-6099) at 929-A Edgewater Boulevard for drinks and dinner with an Irish accent. Reuben's (415/574-8330) on 3025 Clearview Way serves dinner and drinks with a clear view. Perhaps the new Metro Center will have a penthouse restaurant with a wider view when you arrive.

Redwood City Shoreline

Since **Redwood City** lost Marine World Africa USA to Vallejo, the Redwood Shores development has been busy replacing the area where whales and dolphins once performed with homes and huge new office buildings. Across from this activity, reached by Bridge or Dolphin Parkway, is the Marina Park development, peppered with small water-oriented parks. But the terns don't want you on their shoreline and most homeowners don't either.

However, a few small parks welcome the public, like **Portside and Starboard parks** on either side of a graceful bridge off Bridge Parkway, or **Marlin and Dolphin Parks** touching on Belmont Slough. Slightly larger **Mariner Park** at the end of Bridge Parkway faces on Steinberger Slough.

Welcome to Pete's. Redwood City possesses several marinas, but a local small boat owner would probably first think of friendly **Pete's Harbor**, with its palm trees, moorings and facilities for small boats, a sailing school, yacht vendor, and more, jammed up against Redwood Creek and Smith Slough.

The hub of all the salt-seasoned comings and goings is Harbor House (415/365-1386), a restaurant designed and built by Pete Uccelli, the owner, who also created the twenty-six-acre complex. This come-as-you-are eatery is open seven days a week for breakfast, lunch (including burgers), and dinner; there's a small wait in the late afternoon after the cafeteria part closes and before sit-down dining starts. Harbor House also harbors Al's Marine Store, which sells gifts and gadgets besides hard-line chandlery items.

How to reach Pete's? Take the Whipple Road exit off Highway 101 and avoid being hurled back on the freeway by turning south on East Bayshore Road. Go past an out-door theater and then bump your way bayward to Pete's parking lot, where you'll see cars wearing bumper stickers that say, "I (love) Pete's Harbor just as it is." As you leave Pete's Harbor a sign advises: "You are now entering the United States. Arrivederci."

The **Peninsula Marina,** next south, has more berths and more manicured landscaping and parking than Pete's, but a certain ambience is missing.

Redwood City also has the South Bay's only **deep water port**, thanks to periodic dredging of Redwood Creek by the Army Corps of Engineers. You reach the port and **marina** by turning near the intersection of highways 84 and 101 at Seaport Boulevard and continuing to the end. Across the channel you see a mountain of stockpiled salt, waiting to be shipped out. Although this is the main cargo now, 100 years ago the port shipped mainly redwood logs.

This is peaceful boat-watching territory, and now there are **walkways, a parcourse and a grassy park** along the channel before the new Portside development. On occasional benches and piers you can sit and watch the pleasure boats slide by. A few people hooked on fishing try off one small pier. Across the channel, half-hidden by dredges and looking somewhat like a misplaced hangar, is the famous "spy barge," once owned by Howard Hughes. Since it's on an island and off limits, it's as reclusive as its late owner.

Charley Brown's (415/364-2848), jutting out over the water on piers, is the only restaurant, although a small store under the Harbormaster's Office sells pop.

Palo Alto and Its Nature Interpretive Center

A generation of children and adults have discovered the world of the salt marsh through microscopes, movies, bike rides, and nature walks at the **Lucy Evans Baylands Nature Interpretive Center** on Embarcadero Road in Palo Alto. This striking Center, built on fifty pilings, was named for the late conservationist, known as "Baylands Lucy," who kept stressing the vital need to protect these 120 acres as a nature preserve for birds and humans.

Besides indoor displays and an open deck, a **wheelchair accessible boardwalk** leads out into the marsh and open water. Here you get an overall view of the plants that thrive in a salt marsh and come within close-up camera range of many **shorebirds**, including the elusive California clapper rail, which is forced out into the open at high tides.

As if this isn't enough, **hiking, jogging, and biking trails** wind through much of this preserve. One goes east from the Center to San Francisquito Creek, turns south, then loops around the **golf course** past the Palo Alto Airport on Embarcadero Road. A longer loop starts to the north and curves south along Charleston Slough. When the slough ends by the Mountain View Shoreline Park, bikers can continue to the edge of East Bayshore Road, then pedal north to the Center on Embarcadero Road.

Any time, during daylight hours, you can savor this open space, so close to crowded Silicon Valley. The Center is open by reservation (415/329-2506) for environmental programs Wednesday through Friday afternoons. Weekends from ten to noon and one to five, anyone can drop in. If the building is closed, you can use the boardwalk; a small **lagoon** near the parking lot always has ducks and geese waiting for crumbs. Also, the picnic and recreation area planned to replace the Palo Alto Marina, which was closed after a bitter legal tussle, may be in.

SOUTH BAY SHORELINE of ALAMEDA & SANTA CLARA COUNTIES

Mountain View and Sunnyvale

In addition to a **golf course** and the nearby **Shoreline Amphitheatre** with its two tentlike roofs (one wag called them the world's largest brassieres), a highlight of the 544-acre **Mountain View Shoreline Park** is a charming saltwater **lake**, fifty-four acres of sparkling water that attacts skippers of small boats and colorful **boardsails**—but no swimmers. One-day vacationers **sunbathe** or **picnic** on the grassy shore as others fly **kites** in the meadows. The historic Rengstorff House was moved to this lakeside area; hopeful plans call for it to be renovated as a **youth hostel**.

As enticing are the park's many **wildlife areas** and more than **seven miles of paved and graded levee-trails** for walking or pedaling along Mountain View Slough and tidal marsh, Stevens Creek tidal marsh, and the Charleston Slough. Eventually you connect with salt marshes near the Baylands Interpretive Center in Palo Alto.

All this outdoor recreational bounty, in the midst of high-stress civilization, is just a mile away from Highway 101. Exit north on Stierlin Road to the gatehouse, where you'll be given a map. You can also reach the park on foot or bike from the north end of San Antonio Road. Call the shoreline office at 415/966-6392 for overall park information or 415/961-7965 for specific information on sailing and equipment needed.

On maps **Sunnyvale Bayland Park** shows as a sizable rectangle of green park west of Alviso and east of the Moffett Field Naval Air Station. This isn't a conventional park yet, although there's a grid of over four miles of **hiking and bicycling trails** on levees along Sunnyvale and Guadalupe sloughs. To get there, turn north off busy Highway 237 at Borregas Avenue, follow your nose to the sewage treatment works, and park in the small lot. Keep dogs and children out of nearby drainage ditches which may contain water that the sewage plant will treat again. If you continue walking or bicycling towards the Bay, with its breezes, the water changes color and the smell of the sewage plant fades away behind you. One advantage of this park is that you should be able to avoid crowds here.

Historic Alviso

The tiny town of **Alviso** has been almost gobbled up by San Jose, and industrial "parks" move ever closer. When you see the handful of boats stuck in the mud at the tiny marina, it's hard to realize that in the early and middle 1800s Alviso was a busier shipping port than San Francisco. In *Two Years Before the Mast*, Richard Henry Dana described how large boats manned by Indians from the missions would bring hides to the vessels.

The nautical blue South Bay Yacht Club still hoists its flag, but about the only marine action now in Alviso is when canoes or shallow draft boats are launched from the tiny **public pier** at high tide. Why? Dredging the constantly encroaching silt in the slough is presently on hold; birds have won over boats. A weathered note on the bulletin board at the large restroom by the marina pleads for dredging to resume. "Without access to the Bay," it continues, "this could turn into the Sahara Desert and boaters might as well take up camel driving."

Alviso also has the bad luck to be flooded every few years when water breaches the surrounding levees. These were built after wells removed so much underground water that parts of the town sank as much as ten feet. No wonder several historic buildings are near collapse. In fact, the old brick pickleworks by the levee on Hope Street may have done so before you arrive. Several Victorians survive, including an ornate 1887 home and the fading wooden building that once housed Laine's Grocery. Both are near a small **railroad station**, built in 1904 and now a private residence.

Another survivor is the colorfully painted old Bayside Cannery at 1290 Hope Street, where the **San Francisco Bird Observatory** (408/946-6548) carries on a program of understanding and protecting the Bay's wildlife through research and education. Swallows nest in the eaves of the funky old building, ducks waddle by, and egrets land in a nearby pond. Just outside, towards the slough, **birders** stroll along the levee trails, since this part of the refuge is incredibly rich in birdlife. When the tide goes out, sit quietly on the tiny pier to get close to many varieties of birds rushing about and feeding on the mudflats.

Sections of present-day Alviso have the ambience of a **ghost town**, but the village of **Drawbridge**, three miles due north along the railroad tracks, is so deserted the ghosts have left. This once-popular hunting resort, which could only be reached by boat or train, is slowly sinking into the mud of the marsh. In its heyday it boasted more than eighty homes, two hotels, and many gun clubs. Now you can see the remains of less than twenty-five buildings. Southern Pacific trains still whistle through, but they no longer stop, and the one remaining drawbridge over Mud Slough is rarely opened. Although Drawbridge is off limits to the public, naturalists from the San Francisco National Wildlife Refuge lead walking tours there. Reservations are needed (415/792-0222), although you can sometimes take advantage of last minute cancellations.

Bulldozers are already busy at the inland edges of Alviso. When the flooding is corrected, Alviso might become modernized. So do visit the present funky town soon. From Highway 101, turn east on 237; from Highway 880, turn west on 237. Drive northwest on Taylor Street and find your way over the railroad tracks to the miniscule downtown area.

Where to eat? Vahls (408/262-0731) at 1513 El Dorado is the fanciest for Italian fare or seafood. If Alexander's is open, you can join many locals for breakfast and lunch. The Marina Bar and Restaurant (408/262-2563) at 995 Elizabeth provides an attempt at a view. If you don't require linen napkins, you could try Rosita's on Taylor for Mexican food (408/262-4350).

At the edge of Alviso, within the jigsaw border of the **San Francisco Bay National Wildlife Refuge**, is the beautiful **Environmental Education Center** (408/262-5513). Besides classrooms, an observation tower, and displays, it overlooks exciting wildlife habitats; here you may see birds and animals you've met only in books or on the television screen. Alviso is at the remote south end of the Bay, and the Center, at the end of Grand Boulevard, is even more remote.

On weekdays teachers and others lead field trips from the Center; on some weekends there are nature programs for the public. If you're not on an official field-trip, you can still drive out, park, and walk along the short boardwalk or on the miles of levee trails. Who says marshes and mudflats are dull and drab? You're surrounded here by a kaleidoscope of greens and earth tones; you'll also discover that the air has an aliveness that's invigorating.

San Francisco Bay National Wildlife Refuge

For an exciting chance to meet wildlife that has survived concrete and shopping malls, be sure to visit the huge **San Francisco Bay National Wildlife Refuge**,

Alviso's Environmental Education Center looks out over miles of marshes and mud flats.

administered by the U.S. Fish and Wildlife Service. Surprisingly, too few people find their way to this precious open space in the heart of a great metropolitan area; it's one of the most under-used natural areas around the entire Bay.

Yet this valuable refuge contains open water, mudflats, salt marshes, and ponds, in addition to drier inland hills and fields. This means you might see a golden eagle and a belted kingfisher within camera range of each other. Black-necked stilts, willets, shovelers, avocets, great blue herons, busy little least sandpipers, and mallard ducks are among the hundreds of other winged visitors to look for. You'll see and hear many on the self-guided **Tidelands Trail** that starts just outside the refuge Visitor Center. You might also glimpse a rabbit or a fox disappearing into the brush.

To get to the refuge headquarters in Fremont, take the Dumbarton Bridge/Route 84 turnoff from Highway 880. Watch for the Thornton Avenue turnoff and follow signs. Before you start out on the six-and-a-half miles of trails in this isolated wildlife refuge, stop in at the **Interpretive Visitor Center**, open 10 A.M. to 5 P.M. seven days a week; closed on all national holidays except Memorial Day, July Fourth, and Labor Day.

Pause first at the outside viewing area to look out over the salt marshes and Bay; inside, from the Center's balcony, the view is even better. The Center's displays introduce you to plants, animals, and birds you may see, although the tiny, endangered pocket-size salt marsh harvest mouse is hard to spot. A small bookstore sells nature guides and you can pick up free maps and brochures. On weekends naturalists lead public nature walks; during the week they're busy with onsite school programs. Call 415/792-0222 for information.

Besides **hiking, bicycle riding, bird watching, and photographing** on the trails, you can fish off a 2,000-foot-long **deepwater fishing pier**, converted from the east end of the old Dumbarton Bridge. (Its twin is on the west end of the bridge.) The road to the pier starts from near the Center parking lot and parallels Highway 84 towards the Bay. During daylight hours, you can walk out a healthy distance to drop your line into forty to fifty feet of water at high tide, twenty feet at low tide. There's also a platform so you can get closer to the water. You can land shark, surf perch, jacksmelt, starry flounder, and bat rays; you might even catch a sturgeon or striped bass. The pier has a restroom, benches, drinking fountain, and fish-cleaning stations. But all is not perfect. To say it's breezy out there is an understatement; sometimes the wind is strong enough to blow off a toupee.

In 1972 Congress authorized 23,000 acres for the San Francisco Bay Wildlife Refuge. It has not reached that size yet, and a Citizens' Committee to Complete the Refuge (415/493-5540) believes at least 10,000 acres more should be added before the wildlife is fully protected. This may seem like a lot of property when the tenants are mainly birds—although the bird population is just a fraction of what the Bay's marshy shores sheltered when the first settlers arrived and clouds of birds darkened the sky. Why protect smelly old salt marshes? Aren't airports, highways, marinas, and housing projects more important? After all, they create jobs.

Don't tell this to anyone who has studied wetlands. One vital purpose of the San Francisco Bay National Wildlife Refuge is to demonstrate the value of open, undeveloped Bay shores, especially marshes. Instead of being drab wastelands to be "reclaimed," salt marshes, acre for acre, are ten times as productive for plants and animals as the most successful wheat farms. "If we destroy wetlands, we bite the hand that feeds us," a park brochure states, "for we destroy the nurseries for many of the fish for our table." As for mudflats, a double handful of San Francisco Bay mud may contain 40,000 tiny living creatures that will feed millions of small animals like clams and fish, which will be eaten by great flocks of birds and large animals like seals—and us. To say nothing of how shoreline marshes help cleanse wastes and toxic chemicals from the water.

Add to this the muted beauty of the Bay's marshes, where—in relative isolation—we can savor peace and quiet and, if we are patient, glimpse the primeval chain of life from our beginning. That alone is worth saving all the wetlands we can.

Coyote Hills Regional Park

Quiet **Coyote Hills Regional Park** is rich in natural beauty, Indian history, and outdoor recreational opportunities. And its 1,021 acres are often sunny. How to get there? From Highway 880 take the Dumbarton Bridge/Route 84 exit west to Newark Boulevard, then right to Patterson Ranch Road, and left to the park's entrance.

In this park's open fields, grassy hills, marshes, and woods, the odds are excellent that you'll meet four-legged wild creatures, from deer and rabbits to more exotic varieties.

As for **birds**, the park lists over 250 species. During their winter migration they rest and feed here by the hundreds of thousands. You can see and hear many on the trail around the freshwater pond or from the boardwalk that meanders through the marsh. En route you'll hear the whisper of wind, the raucous honking of ducks, the

Miniature airplane buffs at Coyote Hills with salt marshes beyond.

melodies of meadowlarks, and the cry of the hawk—perhaps a marsh hawk scanning the tall, rustling cattails. At the pond's edges, great egrets or great blue herons stand motionless, waiting to spear fish. In the willows near the entrance gate, black-crowned night herons doze.

In the early days most of this land was under the Bay; the shoreline was near the park's eastern boundary and the Coyote Hills were islands. For more than 2,000 years, **Ohlone Indians** lived here. The Visitor Center displays a few of their baskets. According to legend, the Indians could weave baskets out of poison oak twigs and not be harmed, yet the few early Russians who confiscated these baskets became stricken with itching misery. The Indians' main legacy here are four **shell mounds** built up mainly by debris from their shellfish diet. Park naturalists lead trips to the largest mound, thirteen feet high; call 415/571-4967 for times.

After this area became part of the Spanish land grant Potrero de los Cerritos (the pasture of the little hills), the Indian population dwindled and the Bay shoreline retreated as marshes were drained and levees erected for salt harvesting. Trails lead up to the crest of the hills where you can see from San Jose to San Francisco over a mosaic of these salt ponds. On breezy weekends up here, graceful **miniature airplanes** soar, along with hawks and eagles. **Walking and bicycling trails** crisscross the park. If these aren't enough for you, check the Visitor Center to find out if trails on the salt pond levees along the Bay are open.

Alameda Creek Regional Trail

Alameda Creek was once the boundary between the 17,000-acre Rancho Arroyo de la Alameda, granted to Jose de Jesús Vallejo and the 30,000 acres of the Mission San José de Guadalupe, dedicated in 1797. As suburbia crept in, much of the creek was concreted in by the Army Corps of Engineers as a flood control measure.

The present wide, level **Alameda Creek Regional Trail** that runs along the south side of the creek is used by **marathon runners**, since cars are not allowed. It's also great for **hiking, bicycling, and wheelchairs**, too. There are pleasant vistas and birds pose at intervals, especially near the Bay. The north side of the channel is reserved for **horseback riding**. Those without steeds can rent one at the Equestrian Center (415/489-2070) near Lowry Road and Newark Boulevard in Fremont.

The trails start far inland at the Vallejo Mill Park in **Niles**, the pre-Hollywood movie capital, where stars like Charlie Chaplin and Gloria Swanson got their start during World War I. About nine miles west, if you're out for a really long run, after you duck under thirteen busy underpasses, you can turn in to the three-and-a half-mile loop trail in Coyote Hills Regional Park. The three additional miles back along Alameda Creek to the Bay's edge total sufficient mileage for an official marathon run.

If you're not feeling that athletic but want to enjoy a dollop of nature, you can connect with the Alameda Trail at many parking places: near Hesperian Boulevard and Lowry Road; Hop Ranch Road; or Decoto Road or at the Jamieson Quarry, both north of Paseo Padre Parkway.

Hayward and San Lorenzo Shoreline

The attractive new **Hayward Shoreline Interpretive Center** (415/881-6751), near the San Mateo Bridge toll entrance, is now open Tuesday through Sunday. To reach it, take the Clawiter Road exit off Highway 92 and turn west on Breakwater Drive to the end. Suspense was high for over a year in 1985 and 1986 when a neighboring property owner closed the only channel that connected the Bay to the eighty-two-acre saltwater marsh here. Finally enough money was found to cut a new channel. Now the many birds who visit here, especially in the winter, will have their marsh back.

To reach the **West Coast's largest restored salt marsh**, continue to the **Hayward Regional Shoreline** at the end of Winton Drive off Highway 880 (old 17). Park near the San Lorenzo Regional Trail entrance just south of your destination. Plans call for a nature center, big recreation area, and restored freshwater pond. Although much work has already gone into transforming this former garbage dump and salt processing area, much needs to be done. However, when grass and native plants heal the scars of its previous life, it will look more parklike.

The area map put out by the East Bay Regional Parks mentions picnicking "on a casual basis, since there are no picnic tables; but lots of space to sit down and watch the water." You can also watch big, bounding jackrabbits. At present some visitors try **fishing** from the levees. Others **jog or hike** along several somewhat rough trails, including the three-mile loop trail around the restored marsh. **Bird-watchers** come for two reasons—to view the shorebirds along the Bay's edge and also the birds that are reclaiming nesting and feeding habitat on the marsh.

This 200-plus acre marsh was restored from a salt evaporating pond started in the late 1800s. In May of 1980 the outward levee was breached to allow San Francisco Bay tides to flow in and out as they had in centuries past. Since then, marsh vegetation has gradually returned. The subtle changes that are taking place in the plant, bird, and animal life make this shoreline an interesting place to visit again and again—that is, if you don't mind what the East Bay Park people call the park's "casual basis."

The **San Lorenzo Regional Trail** runs north from the Hayward Regional Shoreline for several miles. Some day it will continue north to San Leandro's many shoreline parks and marinas. As it is now, it's used for **biking, hiking, and jogging**, and there's one area where collectors can dig up old bottles. You can reach the trailhead at the end of Winton, as already mentioned. Amenities here include a primitive restroom. The paved part of the trail runs along a creeklike body of water by a field where apprehensive cattle graze. Almost at the shoreline the smooth paved area ends; to continue take the dirt trail north.

If you collect **old bottles**, head immediately towards the shoreline near a short bridge. First you'll notice the green, purple, and amber of broken glass along the creek's edge. Along the Bay's edge here at minus tide you can join dedicated collectors digging a foot or so down into the mud to retrieve old whiskey, medicine, mayonnaise, and other bottles that survived the late dump. Mucking about in mud may not be everyone's idea of fun, but how many places can you dig for treasure with shorebirds watching a few feet away and, on clear days, see the skyline of San Francisco in the distance?

You can also reach the San Lorenzo Trail from the end of Grant Street. Take the Lewelling Boulevard turnoff off Highway 880, which puts you briefly on Hesperian. Almost immediately turn westward on Grant, which ends at the San Lorenzo Sewage Plant. You can park in the small fenced East Bay Park's lot and walk north along **San Lorenzo Creek**. If the tide is out, you'll see the Bay over a wide expanse of tirestudded mudflats. You can enjoy this scene from one solitary bench on the south side of a short bridge or from one picnic table on the other side.

San Leandro Marina, Shoreline Parks, and Marsh

The present city of **San Leandro** is a far cry from the 1850s, when squatters tried unsuccessfully to take over the Rancho San Leandro of José Joaquin Estudillo. From 1855 to 1872 it was the seat of Alameda County and called itself the Cherry City of California. Now, instead of cherry orchards, the city can point with pride to the **San Leandro Marina** and all the recreation along its shoreline.

Take the Marina Boulevard exit west off Highway 880; follow it to the end, turn on to Neptune Drive and park near whatever recreation you prefer. **Golf?** On the inland side is the nine-hole Marina Golf Course, and farther on the eighteen-hole Tony Lema Golf Course. The area towards the Bay is taken over by the marina, which is sizable enough to have two yacht clubs, the Spinnaker and the San Leandro. **Windsurfing lessons** are offered and on the south side of the marina is a public **boat launching ramp** and a free **fishing pier**. You can also try your luck along the rocky shoreline if you have a fishing permit.

The harbormaster's office (415/577-3472) overlooks a man-made lagoon crowded with ducks and seagulls who often rest on small wooden islands. Benches and picnic tables are scattered along the Bay south to another small **shoreline park** at Mulford Point. Here a colorful mosaic wall recalls the turn of the century when this was originally Mulford Canal. The San Leandro oyster beds flourished then, often preyed upon by oyster pirates like Jack London. Besides water birds and a plethora of pigeons, you can watch "big metal birds" land or take off from the nearby Oakland Airport.

Just to the south is yet another portion of the park, with another pier, a parcourse, playground, **horseback riding** trail, and plenty of **picnic spots**. A levee with natural open space curves out into the harbor trails for joggers or horseback riders.

If you're hungry or thirsty, don't worry. The Blue Dolphin (415/483-5900) has acres of free parking and can seat 1,000. Horatio's Restaurant (415/351-5556) is close to Neptune Drive and the Marina Inn. Other restaurants include the Casa Maria and another eatery is scheduled to open nearby.

In the 689 acres of the **San Leandro Bay Regional Shoreline**, north of the airport, you'll discover a dozen ways to enjoy the outdoors, and most of them— even shoreline **hiking and jogging trails**—are geared for **wheelchair access**. As another plus, this recreation area is easy to get to. Coming from Alameda, continue south on Doolittle Drive to Swan Way. To reach the eastern edge from Highway 880, take the 66th Avenue exit or the Hegenberger Road exit, turn on Edgewater Drive and go to the end. To get to the main portion from 880, take the Hegenberger Road turnoff and go north on Doolittle Drive to Swan Way as above. Then follow signs.

The park has two free parking lots with restrooms, grassy picnic locations, and plenty of turf for games. At the northern area, closest to the wildlife action, you get sweeping views of Oakland, the East Bay hills, and downtown San Francisco from the top of the Visitor Center's **wheelchair accessible ramp**.

Seagulls at The Beach Cafe in San Leandro.

For **birders**, a boardwalk reaches out into **Arrowhead Marsh** to give you a close-up view of resident and migrating winged wildlife. At the turn of the century there were 2,000 acres of tidal marsh around San Leandro Bay. Today only 70 acres of salt marsh remain, which makes it invaluable to birds. In the spring many are in their breeding plumage: avocets, stilts, willets, and curlews, to name a few. As a special thrill, within camera range, after a very high tide, you're likely to see great blue herons and worried, soft brown clapper rails, driven to high hummocks to wait until the tide recedes. Interested in fishing? From the square **fishing pier** nearby, you might bring in striped bass, salmon, jacksmelt, surf perch, white croaker, sturgeon, leopard shark, and flatfish.

There's another slice of the park to the west, across San Leandro Bay off Doolittle Drive. It, too, has picnic facilities plus a **boat launching ramp**. The Beach Cafe Restaurant (415/638-0307), actually a cafeteria, serves breakfast, hot dogs, burgers, or a lunch special (until 4:00 P.M.) which you can eat inside or on the deck overlooking the water.

Gulls and mudhens congregate here, but farther along Dootlittle Drive in **Doolittle Pond** you might see a half-dozen great egrets convening together. The pond is just west of the small **model plane field** and kitty-corner from the Alameda Municipal **Golf Course**. However, parking is almost nonexistent and there's talk of running a wide road through here. If that happens, Doolittle Pond might disappear, so visit it now.

OAKLAND
&
ALAMEDA
WATERFRONTS

Sunny Alameda

Alameda calls itself an "island home town." Although it snuggles up against Oakland, with whom it shares the busy Embarcadero and harbor, it retains a quiet, turn-of-the-century feel. Yet this island is far from isolated. You can reach it easily coming north on Highway 880 (old 17) by crossing over Oakland's inner harbor on the High Street Bridge, the Fruitvale Bridge, or the Park Street "lift" bridge. Farther north you can arrive at Alameda through the Posey Tube.

If you've been investigating the San Leandro Bay shoreline on Doolittle Drive (Highway 61), going north you pass the Alameda boundary at the Alameda Municipal **Golf Course** near a **model airplane field**. Turn left on Island Street and right on Bridgeway and you're on **Bay Farm Island**. What's there besides a huge housing development? You can jog or bicycle on a bayside trail while airplanes thunder overhead at **Shoreline Sea View Park**. Continue on Bridgeway and go right on Auginbaugh Street to the end. Long-time Alameda residents who watched Bay Farm "Island" building up remember when you had to pause on the road to let families of ducks cross. No more.

If you don't make that turn to Bay Farm Island but stay on Highway 61 instead, you cross a bridge over by the small Aeolian Yacht Club to the "real" Alameda island. Highway 61 eventually reaches the Posey Tube. On weekends a gigantic **flea market** draws crowds to the outdoor theater area here. (415/522-7206)

Just before the entrance, turn east on the Mariner Square Loop, and you're in **Marina Village**, one of the many complexes that cater to the owners of Alameda's 2,700 boats (the Navy and Coast Guard, who own much island real estate, own many boats, too). At Marina Village you can buy a new yacht, admire sailboats, learn to sail or partake of grog and grub at the Rusty Pelican (415/865-2166) or the Barge Inn (415/522-3325), near an assortment of houseboats.

To reach the Alameda Marina at 1815 Clement Avenue, turn off Highway 880 at the 23rd Avenue exit, then cross to Alameda on the Park Street Bridge and go right on Clement. Take the same exit and the Park Street Bridge to the Alameda Yacht Harbor at 1535 Buena Vista Avenue.

Another yacht harbor, this one with a minipark, is at **Ballena Bay**, on the opposite side of the island. From the Posey Tube take Webster to Central, go west to Ballena Boulevard, and turn left. A **boat launch** is by the breakwater, which doubles as a primitive fishing pier. For fine dining, there's the Whale's Tail (415/865-7552). For French cuisine, inside or outside around a swimming pool, there's the Beau Rivage (415/523-1660)—better make reservations and bring a credit card.

Many visitors not lucky enough to have a yacht berthed in Alameda head for **Robert W. Crown Memorial State Beach**, open daylight hours. Take Webster Street to Central Avenue (as above), go left two blocks to Westline Drive, then right on Westline to the entrance. Besides **two-and-a-half miles of sandy beach** that is shallow and warm enough for **swimming** (without a lifeguard, however), 383 acres of green grass, picnic tables, and freshwater lagoons await you. An interpretive **Visitor Center** (415/521-6887), open March through November, has displays and programs to help all ages learn about the Bay and its wild inhabitants. The center also sponsors a **sandcastle building contest** in June.

If the visitor's center is closed you can still **stroll the beach, hike, jog, picnic, throw horseshoes or volleyballs, fly kites, and try the exercise course**. During low

A Crown Beach ranger teaches children Indian skills.

tide at the cove, now a **protected marine reserve**, you can see (but not remove) many creatures that live between the tides.

In the late 1800s, before its metamorphosis into Crown Beach, this was Neptune Beach, a Coney Island–style park where thousands rode roller coasters or merry-go-rounds or dallied in the 300-foot-long saltwater plunge. During World War II, naval cadets trained here. In 1955 sand was dumped onto the mudflats and in 1959 the beach became a state park. However, 1981 storms removed most of the sand. With $2.5 million worth of sand deposited along the beach, there's now enough shore to relax, picnic, or **sunbathe** on, with San Francisco as a backdrop. You can also walk out on a narrow breakwater for a wider view.

Close to civilization as it is, this is a prime area for **birders**. Along Shoreline Drive at the park's south end, in the the **Elsie B. Roemer Bird Sanctuary**, you'll meet more than twenty species in the marshy area, from tiny sandpipers rushing about to snowy egrets standing imperiously aloof.

Before you leave Alameda, take time to admire its well-kept-up **Victorian homes**. You see them along streets like Santa Clara and Central; there's a delightful cluster close to shady Franklin Park, near Grand and Sherman streets and Clinton and San Antonio avenues. You can pick up a map at the **Alameda Historical Society Museum**, 1327 Oak Street; call 415/521-1233 to be sure it's open.

Oakland's Embarcadero

If you haven't defected to Alameda, take any Embarcadero turnoff from Highway 880 and discover the **Oakland Embarcadero**. You'll pass a series of shipyards and marinas, interrupted at intervals with landscaped picnic areas and restaurants overlooking the water. But first, there are the bridges.

The late-1930s W.P.A. drawbridge at High Street sports a tiny tower which was de rigueur on bridges built in this period. From here you can glimpse small waterfront houses crowding the shore and rowboats, as well as motorboats, out for a spin. Almost under the Fruitvale drawbridge, next north, are two **fishing platforms** with benches where the rod-and-reel set tries to catch striped bass and perch.

Lively Pier 29 restaurant (415/261-1621) is at the eastern foot of the Park Street bridge. Its official address is 300 Twenty-ninth Avenue, Oakland and, although it's jammed right next to the bridge, it has a romantic glassed-in area overlooking the channel dredged to make Alameda into an island. There are also glass windows in the floor in case a mermaid swims by below.

Take the 16th Street turnoff from Highway 880 to the **Central Basin of Embarcadero Cove**. This is a colorful mix of working fishing boats, yachts, Victorian homes moved here to house offices and shops, an actual lighthouse, newly landscaped areas where you can stroll, and interesting vistas and benches where you can sit to enjoy it all. At the turn of the century this was called Brooklyn Basin, and every class of boat from whalers to tramp steamers to ships carrying spices tied up here. Some of that color remains. Although the fishing fleet is not as active as in previous years, fishermen still swap tales in the sunshine or in The Dock Cafe (415/261-1502), the local waterfront eatery. You can join them there to down draft beer or munch a burger.

The Victoria Station (415/532-1430) is in a refurbished railroad car, and the greenhouse dining room looks out over the water. Expect a wait (sorry, no reservations) if you intend to dine at L. J. Quinn's (415/536-2050). It's in a charming 1906 **lighthouse** barged to this location; the view out towards Alameda's Government Island and Oakland would have pleased Gertrude Stein, whose remark that Oakland has "no there, there" is constantly quoted (in this book, too). In a hurry? A second-floor gallery with outside deck dispenses spirits and delifood.

At 1111 Embarcadero, on the **North Basin of Embarcadero Cove**, you can choose from an extensive seafood menu at The Ark, (415/893-5900) and you can dock your boat outside. The Oyster Reef (415/836-2519) at 1000 Embarcadero features barbecued oysters and other seafood.

Along the Oakland Estuary

Since Oakland has one of the world's busiest container ports, even busier than the once proud port of San Francisco, most of its nineteen miles of waterfront are geared for work. Yet tucked among berths, cranes, and terminals are waterfront recreational refuges.

Farthest west is **Port View Park** at the end of Seventh Street on a man-made peninsula sticking far out into the Bay. Coming from San Francisco, take the first turnoff at the West Grand Avenue exit, then the Harbor Terminal exit, then onto Maritime Street, which carries you to Seventh Street. Along the miles of container yards, you'll see and hear the trains, trucks, and whining machinery that accompany this busy activity.

Passengers on a free boat trip along the Oakland Estuary enjoy the view of Oakland's waterfront.

When you notice trees lining the water, you're close. At the park you can **picnic**, assured of drinking fountains and a restroom nearby. If you didn't bring picnic fare, the Oyster Pirate Snack Bar sells beer, bait, hot dogs, and other viands. Be sure to climb up the four corkscrew stories to the top of the park's **observation tower** for exciting close-ups of the Bay Bridge and San Francisco. But wherever you sit or stand you'll see plenty of maritime action. All kinds of boats, from sailboats to huge liners, pass so close you can almost shake hands with the crew.

The octagon-shaped **fishing pier**, open twenty-four hours, is lit all night. But day or night you may have to share your catch with local wildlife. Besides barking sea lions that sometimes climb up on an offshore buoy, brown pelicans often join you in trying for kingfish, perch, flounder, sharks and skates, or the more exotic halibut and bass. Crabs have been caught here, too, and striped bass by the score have been landed on a single night. As a culinary extra, you can cook your catch on a charcoal grill by a picnic table.

Farther east, you can also fish and boat watch off the tiny pier in the miniscule **Middle Harbor Park** at the foot of Ferro Street. Small as it is, it provides water, benches, and tables. From Highway 80, take the same West Grand exit as to Port View Park and follow Maritime Street to Middle Harbor Road. When you see the huge U.S. Lines Terminal zig south across the tracks to Ferro. From Highway 880 go south on Adeline, which becomes Middle Harbor Road, then continue as above.

The small public recreation area at the **Franklin D. Roosevelt fishing pier** is easier to find. It's just west of Jack London Square near the Boatel. You get there by taking the Broadway turnoff off Highway 880 and following signs. This concrete park is dressed up with boxed plantings, benches, a fancy restroom, and a tower where you can observe maritime activities. As at other estuary piers, fishing is exciting when the stripers are running.

There's some talk of adding a small museum. Also, eventually Roosevelt's presidential yacht, the **Potomac**, being reconstructed to its former glory at a nearby shipyard, will be tied up here near the Oakland fireboat, a Pearl Harbor veteran. From the 880 freeway at the 16th Avenue exit, you can see (but not tour) the drydocked *Potomac* which almost ended its life as a drug smuggling boat but was rescued by the Port of Oakland.

Jack London Square

Most people come to **Jack London Square** for the marina and forever-changing restaurants and shops. You can snap a photograph of the log cabin, with its sod roof, where London lived while prospecting for Yukon gold in the winter of 1898. Back in Oakland, when London wasn't following his trade of oyster pirate, he wrote hardfisted adventure tales and drank at funky **Heinold's First and Last Chance Saloon**, built in 1883. Robert Louis Stevenson was another literary luminary who enjoyed the saloon's ambience. Don't worry about the menacing tilt of this tiny watering hole; it's propped up with concrete. Visitors should be warned, however, of the two-way communication between restrooms and bar, which is supposed to titillate the audience.

Bret Harte was also drawn to this brawling area, and like London, used much local lore in his stories. Some of the color of Harte's Gold Rush tales has been captured in the **Victorian homes**, shops, and restaurants along **Bret Harte Boardwalk**, on Fifth Street between Jefferson and Clay streets, in the shadow of the freeway. There's even a restaurant called Eat Your Harte Out.

One of the best deals back at Jack London Square is the **free boat tour** of the port of Oakland if you're lucky enough to get a reservation (415/839-7493). From May through August at ten and noon on Thursday and Saturday, the boat leaves from the Harbor Tours cruise boat dock next to the Grotto restaurant. Passengers see busy terminal activities like "hustler" trucks bringing cargo to the huge gantry cranes. Before returning, the tour boat takes a wide swing out into the Bay.

Where to eat on shore? A small dock probes out between the Metropolitan Yacht Club and the Marina, crowded with sailboats and yachts. You can buy snacks, beer, and other necessities at the tiny Salty Dog at the end or you can bring your own sandwich and sit on a sunny (usually) bench to eat what you don't donate to small birds.

If you prefer restaurant fare, you have a choice of many eating establishments. The closest to this dock is ristorante (small r) Pescatore (415/465-2188), where you can dine on Italian cuisine inside or outside. You also have this option as you eat fancy Mexican food at the nearby El Caballo (415/835-9260) in the Port of Oakland building. Four stories above, reached by an outside glass elevator, the Emperor (415/893-9937) serves Cantonese and Szechuan cuisine and a champagne brunch on Sunday. Even if you're not a fan of Chinese food, the view over the Estuary is worth the price of a cocktail.

The Grotto (415/893-2244), on a pier at 70 Jack London Square, has been serving seafood, steaks, and such since 1936. The newer Scott's (415/444-3456), also on the Estuary and also featuring seafood, counts jocks among its clientele. A scattering of smaller restaurants is a block or so back from the waterfront, along with a welfare office, warehouses, an adult movie house, and other city life fringe benefits.

Jack London Village has more restaurants, but better check to be sure they're still in business. To walk to this sleepy, pleasantly landscaped gathering of tourist-oriented shops, you must wend your way east through a private parking lot until you see the whitewashed (or graywashed) wooden buildings. On the second floor, at a deli overlooking the courtyard, you can relax outside at tiny umbrella-clad tables. Shenanigan's (415/839-8333) overlooks the Estuary. The Wine Garden restaurant and bar is on the first floor. Most facilities, however, ignore or face away from the Estuary.

If the new office building—cum parking garage, retail shops, and restaurants— hasn't been built yet, to reach the next restaurant and pier going southeast on foot you must cross an uneven, debris-strewn empty area past the fancy, fenced-in Porto-bello office and condominium complex to the Rusty Scupper (415/465-0105). Those arriving by boat can tie up at the restaurant's dock. Driving from Jack London Square, take the Embarcadero east. From Highway 880, first take the Jackson Street exit, then the Embarcadero.

South of the Portobello's marina is the manicured seven-and-a-half-acre **Estuary Park** with **picnic tables** under an old-fashioned pergola. You'll also find a drinking fountain, restroom, and **boat launching ramp**. The main enticement is probably the small, square **fishing pier**. Although it barely reaches into the Estuary, enough kingfish, perch, and bass can be caught to help fill up depleted freezers, according to some locals who fish here.

Lake Merritt

You need a boat or water wings to continue on to Lake Merritt, as a tidal channel with shipyards and rusting barges on the other shore blocks the way. In early days this was called the **Estero de San Antonio**; in 1820 Luis Maria Peralta, a sergeant in the Spanish Army, was given title to the 48,000-acre Rancho San Antonio. This property covered most of the East Bay north to the present border between Albany and El Cerrito. In those days, San Antonio creek fed estuary waters inland half a mile to a large, marshy tidal basin, since transformed into landscaped **Lake Merritt**.

In 1866 then-mayor Samuel Merritt earmarked this area for a saltwater lake; some of his fellow citizens built ornate homes around the anticipated shoreline. Finally, in 1907 the Y-shaped Lake Merritt was created, with hydraulic gates to control the water level. In 1909 Mayor Frank Mott bought the land surrounding the new lake; appropriately most of it was named Lakeside Park. From that time on the public has been able to enjoy 160 acres of outdoors in the heart of downtown Oakland. It's a magnet for **joggers**; many circle the entire lake. The birds weren't forgotten either; in 1870 this was named a **wildlife sanctuary**, the oldest in North America.

There's hope that Estuary Park will continue all along the tidal channel to Lake Merritt. At present you're cut off by railroad tracks, fences, and industry. You can drive inland to Lake Merritt on Oak Street just to the west of Estuary Park. This turns into Lakeside which, as its name indicates, gets you to the lake side.

The award-winning **Oakland Museum** (415/273-3401) at Tenth and Oak streets features ecology, art, and history of California. At the lake's south end (the bottom of the Y) you're near the Court House and the Municipal Auditorium. To reach the shore from the auditorium on foot, you must duck into a tunnel under the busy roads bordering the lake. BART has a Lake Merritt stop, but it's a distance from the park.

Close by, one of the great old ladies remaining from the late 1800s, the **Camron-Stanford home**, looks over the sloping green lawn to the water. You can visit it on Sundays from 1 to 5 P.M. to relive its Victorian heyday; it also can be rented for group activitites and weddings. As a precaution, the front door of the Camron-Stanford home is locked; you must ring a bell and enter from the side. This might serve as a reminder. As in all urban areas, it's wise to take care. No swinging handbag or strolling alone at dusk or in the darkness. Enjoy this many-faceted lake, but don't forget your "city smarts."

Lakeside Park, to the north, has something for every taste, including a bandstand and a **horticultural garden** with an herb and fragrance section. Six acres of floral and cactus displays are open daily at the Lakeside Park Garden Center. There's also a fairyland for children (and adults) reached via a toy train.

At the Sailboat Clubhouse (415/444-3807) you can **rent canoes, rowboats, paddleboats, or sailboats**. Another option on weekend afternoons is a ride around the lake on the **Merritt Queen**, a replica of an old Mississippi riverboat, which departs from the Sailboat House. The nearby Rotary Natural Science Center, open every day, displays caged wildlife like burrowing owls, and provides lectures, films, and tours.

A big attraction at this end of the lake is the **wildlife sanctuary** where birds have been protected since 1870. Gulls and ducks by the thousand flock here. Some, like geese, are domestic; many of the rarer birds there were casualties of hunting accidents. Since this is on the flyway, others like the Canada, snow, and white-fronted geese visit from the north. You'll also see pelicans, swans, coots, and all kinds of egrets, from snowy to cattle egrets. Black-crowned night herons and other species nest on a man-made island. A pair of injured Canada geese has also nested there for decades, annually producing young able to fly away.

If you are impressed with the number of birds, wait until the daily feeding, around 3:30 P.M., when the quantity and clamor increases. Then you can get close to usually shy species. Two injured white pelicans, unable to fly, crowd up to the bank to get their share of the smelt tossed to them, and black-crowned night herons fly up in trees to within inches of onlookers' heads. It's great entertainment and, when the show is over, you can stay on to feed the ducks.

Pelicans and seagulls rest at Lake Merritt, which contain's the nation's oldest wildlife sanctuary.

EAST BAY ALAMEDA COUNTY NORTH of the BAY BRIDGE

Radio Beach

As you drive east and north of the Bay Bridge on I-80, the first Bay access appears to be in Emeryville. But **Radio Beach** in Oakland is even closer. In fact, it's parallel to the bridge toll plaza, near radio towers and a cluster of green shacks on wharves. To explore this tiny, little-known shoreline, going west turn off at the last Oakland exit. Instead of a U-turn to the Oakland Army Base, look both directions and take the small one-lane road marked Radio Stations. Going east from San Francisco take the Oakland Army Base turnoff and follow the signs west, as above.

The parking area at the first radio station is thick with no trespassing signs, so find parking off the road. The first sandy crescent of beach is pleasant enough if you can ignore the roar of nearby traffic. A quieter, sandy beach is beyond the private parking lot of another radio station; you reach it by climbing over the low concrete wall.

Most people find their way here to **fish**, but **birders** should enjoy the shorebirds and ducks—thousands rest on sand spits during their migrations. (Those green shacks belong to duck hunting clubs.) You're sure to see gulls and grebes, probably common and Arctic terns, and perhaps the rare least tern. In the small nearby marsh, especially at high tide, you may glimpse the California clapper rails that nest here.

Winds and tides donate piles of **driftwood** and debris to this end of the Bay; some of it originated far inland and hitched a ride on the Sacramento River. During low tides, especially after storms, beachcombers in rubber boots find everything imaginable from firewood to furniture to floats to duck decoys to—you name it, if you can. There's beauty to be found even in debris and mud. A retired teacher who often parks his van here has been driven to attempting haiku to describe the sunset colors on the mirrorlike mudflats. When you leave, retrace your route on the one-lane radio road, and do take the turnoff to the Oakland Army Base where signs guide you onto I-80 going north.

Emeryville Mudflats and Park

Imagine a shoreline people-bird-refuge looking towards San Francisco in com-pact industrialized **Emeryville!** This must surprise old-timers who recall the aroma of paint factories and untreated sewage as they rounded the Emeryville curve on I-80. Wags called it Point Cologne, and many a motorist feared the car's brakes were burning. (Sometimes they were.) Now that most of the odoriferous ambience is gone, motorists speeding along I-80 are usually aware only of Emeryville's wall of concrete and glass buildings and the condominiums out on Emeryville Point, an artificial peninsula in the Bay.

Passersby are also amused by Emeryville's **mudflat sculptures** ranging from fey to actually artistic that students, artists, nearby residents, and unknown benefactors have constructed. Their materials are driftwood, old tires, plastic bottles, hubcaps, and other miscellany of our throwaway civilization. Trains, whole orchestras, boats, and lesser sculptures appear, then disappear under the onslaught of storms and tides.

This outdoor gallery with its debris and freeway noise does not seem to bother the **ninety species of birds** who are inhabitants or visitors. Graceful white egrets patrol; stilts with bright enamelled-on white and black plumage stand on long, thin red legs; terns and gulls wheel in the sky; and sandpipers rush back and forth in

*A sculpture in the
Emeryville mud flats.*

the oozing mud and marshland (which the city prefers to call the **Emeryville Crescent**).

You can see this mixture of art and birds close-up by taking the path off Powell near the freeway fence across from a service station by the Holiday Inn. Good luck parking. If you can't find room on Frontage Road, try the concrete parking garage. For local and transbay buses, call AC Transit at 415/839-2882.

The path above the mudflats is paved the short distance to a **bird observation platform**, where you can relax on a bench as you spot the varieties described on a plaque. The Audubon Society, which furnished this attractive platform, hopes that observers won't trample the fragile mudflat plants or bother the birds during their spring nesting season. If you do venture on farther wear boots, especially near Temescal Creek. If birds are scarce, to the west you're treated to views of the towers and hills of The City.

On weekdays business types and hotel and restaurant guests crowd around the peninsula's highrise buildings. To escape this earnest hubbub, take to the overgrown **jogging trail** that hems the water or continue driving out and around the point to the **shoreline park**. You'll find grass, adolescent trees, benches at scenic intervals, one restroom by a flag pole, and **picnic tables**. Too windy? A walkway fronting the Watergate condominiums has a **glassed-in observation area** where you can look, unruffled, at the hills, Bay, and city.

The park's new-looking **fishing pier** has fish-cleaning facilities and benches. Kingfish, flounder, and perch are sometimes caught here, but anglers are more successful off the rocky riprap Bay edge to the north. Adjacent to the pier, at the shoreline reserved for birds, sandpipers and other shorebirds run by within camera range.

Where to eat? Restaurants on the Emeryville peninsula run the gamut from exotic dinner fare at Trader Vic's (415/653-3400) to Carlos Murphy's (415/547-6766) for moderately priced hamburgers and Mexican food as you look out towards their small public pier. Carlos Murphy's advertises that the "fiesta never ends," but a sign at the entrance promises that they open when they feel like it (around ten) and close when "we have to." Charley Brown's (415/658-6580), which also has a short public pier, attracts the expense-account crowd; it specializes in fish, prime steaks, and cocktails.

The Oceanview Restaurant (415/655-3388) at the tip of the peninsula serves Chinese lunch specials on weekdays and promises a happy hour from 4:30 to 7:00 P.M. before your gourmet dinner. Although there's no ocean view, the Bay view is excellent and so is the food.

Berkeley Marina and Parks

Instead of continuing towards **Berkeley** on I-80, many drivers prefer jolting along the slower frontage road by the rocky shoreline starting at Emeryville; commuters often take this road when traffic ties up the freeway.

The original Berkeley shoreline is east of I-80, around Second Street. The first municipal wharf poked out into the Bay from there in 1908. The hospitable **Montali Winery Tasting Room** (415/540-5551) at 600 Addison occupies the site. Inexorably, as the Bay's edge was filled in—mainly by sanitary landfill, i.e., dumped garbage—the shoreline advanced past submerged tidelands acquired by the railroad empires to areas now wanted for public parks and recreation.

Long, narrow lagoonlike **Aquatic Park** survived being filled in, although when I-80 is widened it may become slimmer. Three main interest-groups use this placid body of water so close to the noisy freeway. The south end, near Ashby Avenue, reserved for the avian set, has a small bird rescue facility (415/841-9086). **Water skiers** zoom back and forth, kicking up spray, in the middle section. They lease a clubhouse and when they fly off the jump here, onlookers get a thrill, too. The north end is for **small boaters** and **windsurfers**; Seabird Sailing (415/548-3730) ministers to their needs. You can reach this end of Aquatic Park, which is also popular with birds, off Addison. There's also an **exercise parcourse** and a ribbon of trail around the lake that's uneven and overgrown.

The Montali Winery, just to the west, as mentioned, offers **free wine tasting**. You can also enjoy a glimpse of Japan and a **free sake tasting** at the Takara Sake factory nearby on 708 Addison.

You don't have to own a boat to enjoy the **Berkeley Marina** at the foot of University Avenue. You'll find restaurants, **walking and jogging paths**, a hotel, **picnic areas, children's playgrounds, a 3,000-foot concrete fishing pier,** and more. Be sure you have a sweater or windbreaker before you investigate these recreational opportunities. Then pick up a **free map and self-guided nature tour** at the Administration Office overlooking the harbor, about halfway out to the pier. There's usually parking space past the Berkeley Marina Sports Center at 225 University Avenue (415/849-2727), which sells beer, bait, hot dogs, and arranges fishing trips.

The most popular attraction out here is that **Berekeley Pier**. At least a quarter of a million people use it every year; when fishing fever hits, hundreds of anglers line the present 3,000 feet of dock trying for smelt, flounders, perch, sharks, skates, rays, and an occasional halibut or striped bass. The pier furnishes fish-cleaning racks and you might find a bench with a windbreak on a weekday. Another attraction is the unkempt restroom at the foot of the dock under the **observation platform**. The views from here are best on a clear morning.

If you take the wind-swept trek to the end, you'll see what's left of an old wooden pier. Its owners, the Golden Gate Ferry Company, built it more than three miles into the Bay to reach deep water. Fishing enthusiasts took over in 1936 when the San Francisco–Oakland Bay Bridge was completed and regular ferry service halted. Nothing has come from nostalgic attempts to restore this ferry service, and controversy rages as to what to do with the nearly two-and-a-half miles of rotting pier at the end; it's been closed since 1955. Should it remain as a landmark and breeding ground for fish or should it be demolished to prevent boats from ramming it?

At the foot of the Berkeley Pier you're sure to notice a thirteen-foot high statue of an angry Chinese God, "The Guardian," shooting an arrow towards San Francisco as he sits astride a "shameless dog." Its creator, Berkeley sculptor Fred Fierstein, impatient of waiting for official Berkeley approval, paid to have his $20,000 sculpture moved here. City officials were unhappy but voters passed a measure to have it kept. Most passersby enjoy the statue. After all, how many times will you see a sculptured dog able to relieve himself? Rain water that collects in the dog's mouth drains through hidden pipes and emerges from the rear of the dog's underbelly.

On the hill directly across from the pier (and statue) and also scattered throughout the Berkeley Marina's 131 acres are **picnic tables**—a few protected from the brisk afternoon winds, almost all sharing that panoramic view towards San Francisco.

South of University Avenue, three small docks and facilities for **water sports** are strung along the riprap Bay's edge near the **Shoreline Park and path**. The Cal Sailing Club (415/527-7245), California Adventures (415/642-4000), and Sailboards Berkeley (415/652-5757) cater to those who venture out on **small boats and sail-boards**. The Bay is a prime location for both sports; beginners have light winds near shore and the experienced enjoy stiff winds towards the middle of the Bay. On a windy weekend you can watch windsurfers of all abilities.

The fenced-in area, just inland, with the large rope spider web and perpetually half-built buildings and boats, is the **Adventure Playground** open from 11 A.M. to 5 P.M. weekends and holidays, and almost every day during the school vacation. Here children can create whatever they want (well, almost) with the wood and tools furnished. For information, call 415/644-6530.

Facilities for those with larger boats are on the harbor side. More than 800 boats can be berthed here; migrating ducks and a live-in pair of loons take advantage of the water in between. The small but private Berkeley Yacht Club, established in 1940, is at the harbor's entrance overlooking breakwaters that provide cormorants a place to dry their wings and gulls and other birds a place to rest. You can enjoy the sights on the path that winds along the shore.

A few **houseboats** off Marina Boulevard near the Marriott Inn tie up at the other edge of the horseshoe-shaped harbor. Go north by the Inn. You can drive or walk towards the Bay on Spinnaker Way past the boat repair and chandlery to a small parking place with a **view of Bay, bridges, and San Francisco**. Walking south

Time out to grab a snack at the Berkeley Pier.

from this parking spot, a short shoreline path ends at the Marina Canteen which offers beer, coffee, T-shirts, a phone, advice, and restrooms.

To the north is the first portion of the **North Waterfront Park** which was transformed from the old Berkeley dump. Eventually the eighty or so hilly adjoining acres, including a protected area facing the Berkeley hills, will also be open to the public. The landscaping is native California plants, courtesy of D.A.W.N. (Design Advocates Working with Nature). Whenever a member is there, you can visit their small nursery off Spinnaker Way, near the boatworks.

Those afternoon breezes? You realize that the landscaping in the North Waterfront Park is comparatively recent when you see the small planted trees struggling to survive hearty afternoon breeezes that often average twelve to fifteen miles per hour. This phenomenon is due mainly to the immense quantities of air breathed out by the central valley. When this valley air warms up, usually around 11 A.M., it rises and pulls in cool, sometimes foggy ocean air through the Golden Gate and up the Sacramento River. The air flows back out around midnight. The result, as most local fishermen can verify, is that early mornings are the calmest times along this shoreline.

When and if the Santa Fe Land company and the city of Berkeley agree, much of the remaining land west of the freeway will be utilized as parkland or development or a combination of both; the drama is presently being played out.

Where to eat? At the end of University at 100 Seawall Drive, Skates on the Bay (415/549-1900) inherited the same superb view as the sorely missed Solomon Grundy's they replaced. H's Lordships Restaurant (415/843-2733), farther south on Seawall Drive, accommodates lone diners or 750 banqueting guests. Some windows overlook the south sailing basin where colorful sailboats and windsurfers ride the waves—and fall in.

The Ayers on the Bay Restaurant (415/845-7656), on University, features New Orleans seafood dinners. The Marriott Inn calls its restaurant The Landing (415/548-7920) and gives you a wide-angle view out over the harbor as you enjoy cocktails, lunch, dinner, or Sunday champagne brunch. If a sit-down meal doesn't appeal, a truck at the foot of the pier sells hot dogs, snacks, and coffee on weekends.

When they want to dine out, many Berkeley-ites head for the cluster of restaurants on or near Fourth Street just inland of I-80. The longest enduring is **Spenger's Fish Grotto** (415/845-7771) at 1919 Fourth. Frank Spenger started this famous enterprise in 1932 as a five-stool cafe next to his seafood market and bait shop; now he has seating for over 700 and sells around 3,000 lunches and dinners daily. If you can stand the often two-hour wait for a table and the incredible din, you will be served crisp French bread and bountiful portions for a surprisingly small tab.

Much quieter and more discreet—so discreet a stranger can hardly find it—is the Fourth Street Grill (415/849-0526), 1820 Fourth, where you should call for a reservation. Informal Bette's Oceanview Diner (415/644-3230) across the street serves breakfast, lunch, and afternoon snacks, plus **steam beer**. Try it!

Albany Waterfront

North of Berkeley and south of Richmond and El Cerrito, the small town of **Albany** boasts a waterfront with an impressive view of three bridges and The City. At present much of this land is leased to Golden Gate Fields for the three-month horse racing season that starts every February. When the lease is up some time around the turn of the century, if the race track moves, this area will probably sprout a shoreline park and development. How much of each has not been decided by Albany and Santa Fe—the current owners.

The Albany **mudflats and tidal areas**, just off busy Highway 580 near where Codornices (Spanish for quail) Creek enters the Bay, are now protected for wildlife. If you train your binoculars there you can see why: **Hundreds of birds** use this area, oblivious to the traffic noise. When CalTrans widens the highway and adds turnoffs, they have promised to supply a bird observation platform so the public can get to know these winged neighbors.

The bulb-shaped peninsula that projects out into the Bay from this area will soon—at least, within a few years—contain a **park, marina, fishing pier, boat launch, trails, and other recreational facilities** open to the public. This is an important step in a long-cherished dream of an East Bay Shoreline Park stretching all the way from Point Isabel in Richmond to the Bay Bridge so that generations to come will enjoy the bounty at the edge of this beautiful Bay.

RICHMOND'S 32 MILES *of* SHORELINE

Richmond's South Shoreline

In the past, **Richmond**, in Contra Costa County, was not famous for greenbelts and parks. The town, started by the Santa Fe Railroad in 1899, has known the smell of oil refineries and the pall of industrial smoke. After World War II, work in shipbuilding and other wartime industries slumped. People moved away and some areas became unsightly. Today all is not perfect, but Richmond does have a surprising number of parks, some high in the hills, many along its naturally air-conditioned thirty-two-mile shoreline. And there's the promise of more.

Perhaps the least endowed of Richmond's edge-of-the-Bay parks—although it has great views of San Francisco and the Golden Gate—is **Point Isabel Regional Shoreline**, named for the daughter of the owner during Mexican days, Don Victor Castro. Yet this small peninsula tip is popular with **bicyclists, joggers, dog walkers, and fishing optimists**—although catches may be suspect because of the highly toxic water.

Point Isabel is easy to reach; Turn off I–80 or 580 at Central Street and drive due west past warehouses and industrial buildings, then north to the end. What's there? You find a few skimpy, shivering trees and areas covered with grass, iceplants, or weeds. One or two benches and picnic tables hide from the brunt of the afternoon winds, which occasional **windsurfers** find pleasurable. What draws many people here is the **paved path**, level enough for **wheelchairs**, that hugs one edge of the park. Watch your step; the path is heaven for dogs, but not for those walking behind. Dedicated **birders** can check the swampy marsh at the unlandscaped east end or the Albany mudflats to the north.

Until CalTrans finishes rerouting it, driving along Highway 580 (old 17) in Richmond is fraught with trucks, bumps, industrial clutter, and red lights. You pass marine industries but glimpse little actual water unless you turn south on Marina Way to the well-advertised **Richmond Marina Bay** development, where newly built condominiums overlook a landscaped **marina-edge park**. Plans call for the two-masted schooner *Jacqueline* moored here to carry passengers on excursions around the Bay. When you check out Marina Bay, the long anticipated restaurant and store may be open.

At present the small blue yacht club at the marina's east end adjoins an area where aged warehouses and former shipbuilding industries were demolished, leaving a bombed-out look.

At the Bay's edge, near a huge piece of concrete that acts as a short pier, an unobtrusive sign promises a **public shoreline** and suggests that you carry out your own garbage. When Santa Fe finishes its grading, you should be able to **hike** along the Bay's edge between Richmond Harbor and Point Isabel. Yes, the present trail is dusty and rutty, and the rocky shoreline is cluttered with debris, but it does have **wide-angle views** and you share it only with occasional birds and fishermen.

Brooks Island, straight ahead a half-mile from shore, is inaccessible at low tide. This undeveloped forty-five-acre island with 360-degree views is off limits, except to groups who reserve through the East Bay Regional Park District (415/531-9300). At present the island is leased to a sportsman's club; the caretaker—on duty around the clock, with watchdogs—leads a Robinson Crusoe existence, sometimes cut off for days by storms and low tides.

There is talk of park-sponsored boat trips to the island if money can be found to rebuild the present hazardous dock. In case that happens, the ancient Indian burial grounds and shell mounds—perhaps the oldest around the Bay—would continue to be off limits. So would the west end of the sand spit where killdeer and black-necked stilt nest, as well as tiny, neighboring Bird Island, used by nesting California gulls, oystercatchers, and Canada geese. But would this fragile island and its native grasses be harmed by too many visitors? Perhaps it should remain accessible only to the birds and other wildlife that need it.

Point Richmond

For higher level (and easier to get to) Bay views, visit **Point Richmond**, the arty village where streets, lined with trees and cosmetically beautiful old homes, climb steeply towards the sky. The turnoff is easy to miss; it's off Highway 580 at Garrard Boulevard.

You know you're there when you see the huge **Richmond Plunge**. For a step back in time, why not look in here? Better yet, take the plunge yourself; call 415/620-6820 for information. This 160-foot saltwater pool, called a natatorium when it opened in 1926, still attracts thousands of swimmers daily. It was a gift of John Nicholl, an early pioneer. When an oil well on his property gushed saltwater instead of oil at 1,232 feet, he presented both property and artesian well to the city.

In downtown Point Richmond you notice that brick is popular. Although you see vacant buildings, more old brick structures are being resurrected. Those already restored include the firehouse, new housing offices, and the 1911 Hotel Mac (415/233-0576), at 50 Washington Avenue, whose interior boasts balconies and stained-glass windows. The menu lists seafood and fettuccine and the "in" crowd keeps the place hopping.

Many visitors, especially yachtspeople who like seafood and Northern Italian cuisine, swear by the Baltic Restaurant and Bar (415/235-2532) at 135 Park Place. Its interior runs to stained glass plus mahogany. For those on a tight budget, the hole-in-the-wall Judges and Spares (415/237-7585), at 130 Washington Avenue, has deliciously low-priced luncheon specials, but don't wait too long or they'll run out.

At 31 Washington, New Whitney's sandwich shop and deli (415/234-7505) is well thought of. As for entertainment, the Masquers Playhouse (415/232-3888), nearby at 105 Park Place, still carries on.

Much of the charm of Point Richmond is reserved for those who walk or drive on the narrow, twisting roads that wind up and up to where the **views** won't stop. Up Washington Avenue to Scenic Avenue to Crest Avenue is one example, but almost everywhere you venture is a delight. You can also approach this hilly area by going through the tunnel near the plunge and taking Western Drive (turn right immediately after you leave the tunnel) and drive on up. When you near the top you'll notice a grassy, open area to the east. This is **Nicholl Nob**, now parkland open to the public. It, too, has panoramic views.

Uncrowded Shoreline Parks and Coves

To reach **Miller-Knox Regional Shoreline**, an East Bay Regional Park open daylight hours, you also go through the tunnel. Its 258 acres contain beachfront, a grassy, landscaped picnic area, and a saltwater lagoon. Just as you exit the tunnel, the small terraced portion to your right is **Keller Beach**, which has an actual tiny **sand beach** where you can **wade or swim** or sunbathe.

Originally Huchium Indians lived along this shore, then Chinese fishermen had a camp. The Santa Fe Railroad, the next arrival, built a dock at the southern tip of the present Miller-Knox Park where you could take a ferry to San Francisco. Long after this practice stopped, freight cars were barged across from this dock. That, too, is no longer, but notice the yard full of metal sculptures just south of the park.

Your route does not end at the off limits petrochemical tanks and buildings south of the park on Garrard; another world awaits to the left at **Brickyard Cove**. There you're in an unusual mix of luxury Riviera-type waterfront homes and condominiums, nearby ships loading steel scrap, a rusty railroad track, and a huge 379-foot PG&E gas tank whose turquoise bulk can be seen from as far away as San Francisco. The historic brick kilns for which this area was named are still there, looking like giant beehives.

Luxurious lagoonside Brickyard Cove homes arrived first at this small, usually balmy inlet that looks out towards Angel Island, Marin County, and San Francisco. The **Richmond Yacht Club** came next. Another developer recently built condominiums that cling to the steep hillside; bulldozers are busy preparing the hillside to the south for more residential living. This latest development will overlook a small freshwater lake and miniscule marsh remaining from old quarry days; it's now popular with red-winged blackbirds. Can casual visitors enjoy this area? They can buy lunch (except on Monday) in the small hexagon-shaped All's Fare eatery. But, no trespassing signs are thick, and parking is not encouraged unless you're shopping for a condominium.

Tiny city-owned **Point Molate Beach Park** is just north of the Richmond-San Rafael Bridge. Turn right just before the toll booths. Ignore the road leading to the new Red Rock Marina; follow the sign to Point Molate and make a sharp left when you see people parked. You can enjoy a sand and pebble **beach**, along with a scattering of **shorebirds**. You'll also find **picnic tables** and **children's play equipment**.

The well-preserved old steam engines and cars in the railroad museum that used to stretch along the hillside across the road had to leave. At last report, the organization was dickering to move to old, unused tracks near Sunol in the Niles Canyon Area. To check, contact the Trans Pacific Locomotive Association, P.O. Box 2465, San Leandro, CA 94577.

After you leave Point Molate Beach Park, Western Drive, the narrow road north, leads you to a getaway so remote you'll have difficulty realizing you're just minutes away from civilization. First the road goes through the Naval Fuel Depot by brick buildings that vaguely resemble castles. Decades ago before the Navy took over—you'll discover from a plaque—these were part of the Winehaven Resort enjoyed by weekending San Franciscans.

A short distance farther, on a dot of an island less than a quarter of a mile off shore, is the photogenic **East Brother Lighthouse**, with its Victorian house, tower, and white picket fence looking like something from a fairy tale. This oldest operating lighthouse on the West Coast now doubles as a bed and breakfast inn, the East Brother Light Station (415/233-2385), from Thursday through Sunday. The price for couples, which includes breakfast and dinner, is expensive, and you have to get used to the sound of the automated fog signal if f-- creeps in. Once the boat deposits you on this tiny rocky island, how you spend your time is up to you, as you're isolated from the pleasures and problems of civilization. The tinier mound of nearby rock, **West Brother Island**, is patronized by birds and barking sea lions.

As you continue on Western Drive towards Point San Pablo (across from Point San Pedro in Marin), the road divides at a small lagoon. The left fork once went to the last **whaling station** on the Pacific Coast. In those days, no matter which

East Brother Lighthouse is now a bed and breakfast inn.

direction the wind was blowing, you could smell the rendering factory. The road is now private, serving the present tenant, which produces dog food, and the oil tanks and other facilities on the hill above.

The right fork turns sharply up the hill towards the remote **Point San Pablo Harbor.** When you reach the first possible place to park, by a locked gate leading to an oil tank, take a short hike up the **steep trail** on the hillside. The view will reward you. Back in the car, a few more twists bring you to the end of the road. If you haven't fallen in a pot hole, you've arrived! The San Pablo Marina is not the St. Francis Yacht Harbor. It is, however, a decided improvement over the semicircle of rotting, sunken boats that once made up the harbor's breakwater. Now small boats come and go, a few imaginative houseboats stay anchored, gulls fly, and party fishing boats ply their trade; Mr. Bass Sport Fishing (415/223-5388) has one boat named *The Happy Hooker.* As for other recreation, a sign on the dock reads, "No Swimming—Fall in O.K."

The Galley Restaurant (415/233-0570) is the harbor's social center. Tuesday through Sunday it sells beer and snacks, breakfast, lunch, and early dinner. Try to avoid arriving at lunchtime; since it's the only restaurant for miles, it's packed then. The settlement lacks even a T-shirt shop, although The Harbormaster (415/233-3224), next door, does sell caps with the San Pablo Yacht Harbor insignia.

Point Pinole Regional Shoreline Park

Don't let the name fool you. **Point Pinole Regional Shoreline Park** is in Richmond, not in Pinole. This 2,147 acres of grassy parkland with eucalyptus **woods, salt marshes, beaches,** bluffs, and a **long fishing pier** edges a portion of the huge Wildcat Regional Park in the East Bay hills. Along this park's shoreline you can escape the fumes of traffic and industrial pollution to **hike, bike, fish, picnic,** and watch hawks and other **birds,** some rare and endangered. You can stroll, jog, or just sit, alone, at the edge of the pebbly shore, listening to the swish-shush of San Pablo Bay as you absorb tranquility and sunshine (probably).

This park inherited the name Pinole because, in 1772, Indians treated grateful Spanish explorers to a porridge of pinole, the Aztec word for toasted or ground grains and seeds.

Point Pinole Regional Shoreline Park is somewhat hard to find. Perhaps that's why it's usually so beautifully uncrowded. From Interstate 80, take Hilltop Drive to San Pablo Avenue and turn right; turn left at Atlas Road. At the park entrance, near Atlas and the Great Highway, you park for a small fee (dogs are 50 cents more) and walk in. If you're headed for the pier, one-and-a-half miles away, you might want to take the park shuttle for a small additional fee. For park information, call 415/531-9300.

How did this 2,147 acres of tranquility escape the bulldozer? Starting with the Civil War, this area—strictly fenced—was used by the Atlas Powder Company to manufacture gunpowder, then dynamite, then nitroglycerine. You can still see bunkers and pits where the hazardous work was done; one huge, grassy pit has picnic facilities out of the wind. For 100 years or so that high, protective fence kept out real estate agents and developers. When nitroglycerine became passé, the Atlas Powder Company sold out to the Bethlehem Steel Company, whose plan for a gargantuan factory never got off the ground.

The park first opened in 1971 as a 161-acre recreational area. Since then, under the umbrella of the East Bay Regional Park District, it grew to cover the entire point. Now from 8 A.M. to 5 P.M. in winter, 8 A.M. to 10 P.M. in summer you can savor its many charms. These include **fishing** for perch, flounder, jacksmelt, kingfish, sharks, and perhaps striped bass or salmon off the **1,225-foot concrete pier** opened in 1977. (The pilings of the old demolished pier, originally used to load explosives, were left to provide a haven for marine life on which many of the fish feed.) You don't need a fishing license to dangle your line off the pier, which is equipped with restrooms and a drinking fountain but no snack bar. So bring your own picnic fare.

Birders should be in luck. Come early, hopefully at a low tide, for best looking. The eucalyptus groves welcome woodland birds not normally found along such a shoreline. Because of the many rabbits and rodents that thrive in the grasslands, Point Pinole also hosts birds of prey like red-tailed hawks, marsh hawks, owls, and kestrels. And, if you're patient, you might spot the salt marsh song sparrow or the California clapper rail.

Even if you don't catch a fish or glimpse a rare bird, at Point Pinole you can escape concrete and cars for a few hours to be healed by woods, wildlife, water, and open meadows. And, when you leave, you can take a sense of its peace with you.

CONTRA COSTA COUNTY SHORELINE

Pinole, Hercules, and Rodeo

Big, beautifully isolated Point Pinole Regional Shoreline Park, described in the last chapter, is actually in Richmond. The town of **Pinole**, not to be outdone, has plans for a small shoreline park near **Pinole Creek**, envisioning grass, a picnic area, and fishing access. But that's in the future.

If you're game, you can reach the present reality by driving to the sewage plant at the end of Tennent Avenue. Take the Apian Way turnoff off Highway 80, go east on San Pablo Avenue, turn Bayward at Tennent, and follow your nose. You can also struggle to the Bay's edge on the creek's side facing **Hercules**. In the days Hercules was a company town run by a powder works, sheep were kept grazing on nearby hillsides to minimize chances of grass fires from powder explosions.

When the Hercules Powder Company moved away, life became less stressful. Now you can watch **birds** in the small marsh, after crossing the busy railroad tracks; there is often sunshine and a clear view across San Pablo Bay. Note the beautiful old Italianate classic house with spacious lawn overlooking the sewage plant. Now owned by a local doctor, it was built in 1894 by Bernardo Fernandez, a Portuguese seaman who arrived during the Gold Rush and became a prosperous merchant.

At present, a well-kept-up **multi-use bicycle trail** parallels Pinole Creek from the Bay to I-80. Hopefully, in years to come, it will stretch to East Bay Regional Parks in the hills above. There's also hope of a shoreline trail reaching west to Point Isabel and the Oakland Bay Bridge and continuing east through Hercules, Rodeo, and onward. This would fill a tremendous need as a recreational safety valve for Contra Costa County's ever-increasing population.

The town of **Rodeo** has a patch of **shoreline access** by its sewage plant and a funky **marina** where you can listen to chickens cackling and ducks honking as you gaze out over boats, sheds, and rusting machinery towards a forest of smokestacks. A coffee shop with a tiny deck is open for breakfast and lunch. If you insist on visiting this marina, turn off I-80 at Rodeo, head toward the Bay until you connect with Pacific Avenue, and drive across a short bridge and down to the water.

Crockett

Instead of hurtling along I-80, a calmer, less-crowded alternative is **San Pablo Avenue**, once the main highway, bottlenecks and all, between the Bay Area and Sacramento. Now this road has moments of calm and, just before you reach Crockett, in the shadow of the **Carquinez Bridge**, you get a cliffside view of the **Carquinez Strait**, that narrow body of water between San Pablo Bay and Suisun Bay.

When paddlewheelers churned the Bay waters, **Crockett** was a busy port. Now it proudly proclaims itself as a town "where time stands still." Take the Crockett turnoff from I-80 to Pomona Street or, if you're arriving on San Pablo Avenue, look for the road that plunges down and under the bridge approach.

The only stoplight in town is on Pomona, the main street. Pomona is somewhat optimistically called the **Avenue of Antiques** because, among others, The Antique Flea, The Victorian, and Another Time Antiques are here. Crockett's most prominent building is the medieval-looking C&H (California and Hawaiian) Sugar Refinery, built in 1906 and very visible on the east side of the Carquinez Bridge approach. Until recently, when sugar became unfashionable, Crockett was a company town and, according to some old timers, life was sweet. Then Crockett was cut loose from the company's apron strings and citizens are wondering what the future will bring . . . or take away.

For the liveliest action in town, visit the small **Crockett Marina** at the southwest end of the Carquinez Bridge. From San Pablo Avenue, drive down the road by the Yet Wah Chinese restaurant and keep turning left. From Pomona Street, turn towards the Bay on Port Road to its end, then left to the unpaved parking area by the railroad tracks. There's a **fishing pier**, but to bring in the really big ones, the Crockett Marine Service (415/787-1047) suggests a half-day to day-long excursion on one of their **party boats**.

The popular Nantucket Fish Company Restaurant (415/787-2233) is here, also, and during balmy weather you can sit outside gazing up at the mammoth silver bridge, as tugs push huge freighters or loaded barges by. Since party boats moor a few feet away, you can get in on the excitement when one comes back with a prize catch of sturgeon or striped bass.

What else can you see in Crockett? Many residents suggest driving on to **Port Costa**, which is tinier than Crockett. Continue east past that one stoplight where Pomona becomes the **Carquinez Scenic Drive**. En route, on your left, Rolph Street leads towards the sugar refinery (not open to the public), a small museum, and an early homestead. Unless you're a hard-core history buff, skip this detour.

Port Costa

Port Costa has been called "remote and sleepy—the perfect tranquilizer." However, the scenic drive to Port Costa from Crockett can be exciting for **bicyclists**, as well as drivers. It skirts a cliff overlooking the Strait so close that sometimes portions of the road fall in. Across this busy waterway, you can see Benicia and other settlements. Close by, pilings and buildings from olden days remain. Then you're funneled through a gap in the hills into Port Costa.

In the 1880s Port Costa was a bustling port where grain was loaded to be shipped out by rail. When modern transportation took over and it became a ghost town, artists and antique shop owners moved in. Then came two bad fires and the passage of time. Port Costa shed many of its craft, arts, and antique shops. Today it's easy to park along Canyon Lake Drive, the main (dead end) street, and grass grows in cracks along the sidewalk.

Perhaps this will change if the 256 acres on the hillside west of Port Costa, recently purchased by the East Bay Regional Park system, become part of the big **Carquinez Shoreline Park**. Perhaps then, too, access to the strait will be easier. At present you have to squeeze through a fence and walk over train tracks to reach the rough shoreline.

Almost everyone ends up in the bulky, brick Warehouse Cafe (415/787-1827) which sells a T-shirt that reads: "Where is Port Costa? Who cares?" When you visit this Port Costa hangout, treat yourself to beer (served in a fruit jar) at the aged bar near a juke box blaring country music. Or you can go outside on a deck overlooking the dusty parking area.

The bar is where you can inquire about Port Costa's lone hotel, the Burlington, which may have finally finished its face-lift by the time you arrive. If hunger pangs strike, the Warehouse Cafe offers barbecued beef or chicken until six P.M. and advertises a lobster dinner on Monday. For full course dining and music that appeals to a different set, try the Bull Valley Inn (415/787-2244) across the street.

Not all antique shops have fled town, and **Muriel's Doll House Museum** (415/787-2820) is still open at 33 Canyon Lake Drive. Muriel displays more than a thousand rag, china, and rawhide dolls, including one that belonged to Sarah Bernhardt. A sign on the door says, "Ring bell; give me time to come down from

Port Costa's main street dead ends at the Carquinez Strait.

upstairs." When Muriel Whitmore does come down and open the screen door, the nostalgia is almost overwhelming. If she is not there, perhaps you'll see her bent figure as she walks slowly down the street talking to a teddy bear she holds in her arms.

What else is there to see in Port Costa? Many residents suggest returning to Crockett. Martinez, with its big shoreline park and marsh and John Muir's home, might be a better bet.

Martinez

Storm damage closed the six-mile scenic drive between Port Costa and Martinez that was compared to the Burma Road or to portions of Monterey's Seventeen Mile Drive. It is unlikely that this route will be reopened to cars soon, if ever. This means that **bicyclists and hikers** can pedal or walk this beautiful road in pristine quiet. However, the drive to Martinez from Port Costa that is open for cars winds through hills scenic enough for anyone. You connect with Highway 4, which has a magnificent view of Mount Diablo, as you go towards Martinez.

Martinez, population around 25,000, was settled in the early 1830s by Don Ignacio Martinez, a Spanish officer who was given land by the Mexican government. When he died in 1849, his eleven children inherited the property. William Smith, a son-in-law, started a trading post here and laid out the town just before the 1850 Gold Rush and Martinez became the county seat. (Early Spanish settlers named the county Contra Costa because it was on the opposite coast from San Francisco.)

The most famous building in Martinez, a well-groomed old mansion with a belltower from which you can see the Strait, is the 1893 **John Muir Home**, now a **National Historical Site**. This is where Muir, the Scottish-born father of our national parks, lived from 1890 until his death in 1914. You can see his desk by a window where he wrote his impassioned pleas to save our wilderness. The site is a mere fragment of the 2,600-acre ranch originally owned by Muir's father-in-law. But the remaining grounds are beautiful, especially when the lush orchards are dusted with blossoms or heavy with fruit.

Muir loved this farm, as he did the mountains. "Climb the mountains and get their good tidings," he wrote. "Nature's peace will flow into you as sunshine flows into trees."

Freeway traffic whizzes by just a short distance away and subdivisions, power lines, and oil industry paraphernalia crowd close, yet Muir's home and eight-and-a-half acres provide an island of green serenity, and the creek cutting through the property is cool and clear.

As a historic bonus, the site also contains the two-story Don Vicente **Martinez adobe**, built in 1844 by Don Ignacio's second son. Although it has survived more than fourteen decades, a posted sign warns that the adobe is not earthquake proof and advises visitors to hurry outdoors if a shake starts. To reach the Muir Historic Site (415/228-8860), open 8:30 A.M. to 4:30 P.M. daily except Thanksgiving, Christmas, and January 1, take the Alhambra offramp from Highway 4 and follow the signs.

The Muir site isn't the only reason to visit Martinez. Other turn-of-the-century homes have survived. So has the Alhambra Cemetery, circa 1851, high on an oak-studded hill. The downtown is well stocked with **antique shops** listed on maps from the **Chamber of Commerce** at 620 Las Juntas Street (415/228-2345).

A "new" site where you can spend many delightful hours, the **Martinez Regional Shoreline** was created from neglected marshland and industrial fill by the city of Martinez and the East Bay Regional Park District. Drive to the end of Ferry Street past the **Amtrak Depot** and across the railroad tracks to this 343-acre oasis.

The western section of the shoreline has quiet open lawns, small family picnic areas, and ponds, all highly populated with ducks, geese, and gulls. The Alhambra Creek wanders through a sizable **saltwater marsh** that has been restored; it's used by shorebirds. Pedestrians can stroll on **miles of trails** through the marsh and along the shoreline.

The eastern portion of the park, run by the city of Martinez, invites group recreation like **soccer and softball**; Joe himself threw out the first ball when the Joe DiMaggio ball field was dedicated. There are, of course, **bocce ball courts**; the game is taken as seriously now as it was in early days, when Sicilians dominated the waterfront population. Near the pier is a memorial to the early Sicilian fishermen— a colorful wooden boat, raised high—with a commemorative plaque.

For **fishing** or ship gazing, try the long, well-lit **pier** reconstructed from the Bay Area's last automobile ferry landing. Moored by the pier is the privately owned 251-foot-long *Fresno*, a steam-powered ferry built in 1927 and retired in 1961 when the **Benicia-Martinez Bridge**, just east, opened. There's still loads of marine action along this narrow waterway, although the **mothball fleet** of war-veteran ships rests on Suisun Bay east of the bridge.

The John Muir Home is a national historic site in Martinez.

Anglers fishing off the pier catch shark, flounder, and occasionally sturgeon or striped bass. The sturgeon catch can be phenomenal, according to local lore, out near the mothball fleet after one of the Coast Guard's periodic attempts to rid the ships of barnacles.

Besides a yacht club, the **Martinez Marina** has a bait shop and party boats. Private boats can use the **launching ramp** for a small fee; call the harbormaster at 415/372-3585.

Where to eat? You don't have to go far. The nearby Albatross (415/228-3800) serves luncheon or dinner with a view out towards the bridge. The La Beaus Bar & Grill (415/372-8941), Marina Vista at Ferry, specializes in authentic Creole cuisine for lunch, dinner, and Sunday brunch. In the downtown area, le cafe (415/229-2442) at Ward and Las Juntas streets offers weekday lunches; dinner Thursday, Friday, and Saturday; and Sunday brunch. The Court Street Cafe (415/228-8366), at 924 Court, is also popular with residents. Martinez has many fast food stops, too. You can find a string of them on Alhambra just north of the Muir Historic Site.

NORTH EDGE of SAN PABLO BAY & CARQUINEZ STRAIT

San Pablo Bay National Wildlife Refuge

As you cross the Petaluma River on Highway 37 going east towards Vallejo, you enter a small, wedge-shaped slice of Sonoma County. Pause if you're avid for **birding**. You're near the 12,000 acres of shoreline and open water in the **San Pablo Bay National Wildlife Refuge**. Hike in less than three miles to **Lower Tubbs Island** and you'll see an incredible number of birds. A good time to visit is in winter when it's cool and the bird population is at its peak.

How did this valuable area escape being subdivided, at least so far? Rather than have it turned into an oil storage depot, the **Nature Conservancy** purchased it in 1969 and donated it to the Fish and Wildlife Service. For information on occasional guided trips to Tubbs Island call 415/792-0222.

If you're on your own, park near the locked gate near marshy Tolay Creek, just east of the Sears Point turnoff to Highway 121 to the wine country. (A U.S. Fish and Wildlife Service sign is inside the gate, along a road and diked trail.) As you walk along past private fields and protected marshlands you'll see coots and ducks, including canvasbacks, bobbing in open water and ring-tailed pheasants in the brush. You should also spot red-tailed hawks and marsh hawks hunting. Since hawks attack when they see prey moving, the large, black-tailed hares (jackrabbits) along the trails have learned to freeze; you may almost step on one before it bounds away.

When you reach an unusual Hansel and Gretel house, erected by students on private land, one trail goes through the marsh and another skirts the Bay. After you hike back and leave this quiet refuge, you can join the honking cars driving east on Highway 37 to Vallejo.

Vallejo's Old Victorians and New Parks

When traffic is light, which it rarely is, **Vallejo** is only thirty minutes from San Francisco. The town's eastern portion along I-80 is wall-to-wall motels and fastfood emporiums. To reach the more scenic Vallejo, turn off at Sonoma Boulevard, Magazine, or Curtola Parkway to the western section, where streets spill down low hillsides to the Napa River before it enters San Pablo Bay.

Vallejo has endured many economic ups and downs since 1850 when Gen. Mariano G. Vallejo donated 156 acres from his 99,000-acre Rancho Suscol to the State of California for a proposed capital. The town was laid out, but the capitol building was unfinished when the legislature convened in January 1852; members had to sit on barrels and boxes. Disgruntled, they left for Sacramento only to return when they were flooded out there the next year; in February, they tried a short stay in Benicia. Eventually they ended up in Sacramento; at last report they're still there.

What kept Vallejo afloat since those early days was building and repairing ships, especially at the huge **Mare Island Navy Yard**. Mare Island—actually a peninsula, not an island—was named for a favorite mare of General Vallejo. The horse was supposed to have drowned but was found grazing on this "island." One hundred thousand workers toiled here during World War II and nearly 400 ships were launched. At present 10,000 civilians work on Mare Island, mainly on nuclear submarines. To take up the economic slack, suburban homes began to "reclaim" swamplands. In the city, waterfront honky-tonks were razed. The Civic Center, a few condominiums, and a park arose on the vacant land.

Then **Marine World/Africa USA** moved to Vallejo, leaving crowded quarters in Redwood City for a new $50 million, 104-acre park with a 55-acre lake. Many—not all—of Vallejo's townsfolk were ecstatic about this entertainment complex, which may lure a million wallet-carrying visitors a year. Hotel developers started making overtures and Red & White ferries (415/546-2896) scheduled runs from Pier 41 at Fisherman's Wharf in San Francisco. As driving and parking can be exasperating, especially on weekends, they also offer a ferry ride/shuttle and admission combination to Marine World, so you don't need to bring your car.

Hundreds of animals, including elephants, giraffes, rhinoceroses, dolphins, and killer whales—one weighing in at 8,000 pounds—had to be moved by trucks or barge more than fifty-five miles to their new home.

The park is open from 9:30 A.M. to 6:00 P.M. There are food concessions or you can picnic under a tree or by the lake. As you enter the gate, pick up a free map that shows where you can get close to animals and exotic birds when they're being fed or showing off their babies. If you sit in the front rows at performances, you may be called on to take part; at water shows you'll get splashed. TIP: Avoid a visit when the neighboring **Solano County Fair** is on, usually in mid-July; the crowds are smaller early in the week and early in the day.

Before you take in other Vallejo sights, if it's a weekday, stop by the **Tourist and Conference Bureau**, i.e. the **Chamber of Commerce** (707/644-5551), at 2 Florida Street north of the new Civic Center. They give out a free town map and four minitour guides to walks and outstanding scenic and recreational spots. Thursday through Sunday, you might visit the 1902 shingled mansion, just north on 1 Kentucky Street. It houses the **Artists League** of Vallejo and shows two floors of members' paintings and handicrafts.

One minitour covers elegant old homes in the **Architectural Heritage District**, designated by brown street signs. Many are clustered along Georgia, Sutter, and Napa streets, on hills overlooking the waterfront. Among the dozens of houses in immaculate shape are 1863 Gothic Revivals, 1895 Queen Annes, and a 1909 home at 728 Capital designed by Julia Morgan. In the 300 block of Virgina, outside this historic district but worth a look, is the Empress Theater, a restored 1930 **art deco movie palace**.

If you're a fan of naval history, just off Capital Street in the former city hall at 734 Marin is the **Vallejo Naval and Historical Museum**. Tuesday through Friday and Saturday afternoon you can review the city's naval career from Mexican days. You'll see historic photographs, ship models, and a working submarine periscope. You can also pick up minitour guides here.

That small grassy park inland on Mare Island Way by the new Civic Center has **play equipment for children, picnic tables, a parcourse, and restrooms**. Across Mare Island Way is **Marina Vista Memorial Park** with a concrete promenade where you can **fish, jog, walk your dog, or bike**. You can also check the passing parade of pleasure boats, with the derricks of the Mare Island shipyard in the background. This is an excellent spot to watch the annual **whaleboat regatta** sponsored by the California Maritime Academy (707/648-4213) in late October.

On Saturdays at 2 P.M. during the summer you can take a ferry trip from the Georgia Street Wharf (behind the Wharf Restaurant) into Carquinez Strait and San Pablo Bay. For reservations call 707/643-7542.

Like to fish? There's a small pier near the **boat launch** area. The longer and more popular **fishing pier** is farther north, almost under the bridge where Highway 37 crosses the Napa River. Take Wilson Avenue that juts off to the northwest from Mare Island Way to the parking area at the end. (There's shade under the bridge.) A small laid-back enterprise dispenses beer, snacks, bait, and advice.

If you're out **birding**, you may see a contingent in the **Napa Marsh** just to the north. To the south is fifty-five-acre **River Park**, which you already passed. Although much of the park dries out into cracked mud during the summer, from the one-and-a-half-mile loop trail you can spot black-crowned night herons, egrets, and other shorebirds.

Besides—or instead of—fishing and birding, you can tour the **California Maritime Academy**, just west of the Carquinez Bridge. Take Sonoma Boulevard off I-80 to Maritime Academy Drive. You'll see how students are trained to be merchant marine officers and can visit the 491-foot training ship *Golden Bear*. Call 707/648-4213 to reserve a tour time.

Where to eat? Many locals head for neighboring Benicia. In Vallejo, the Wharf (707/648-1966), already mentioned, overlooks the water. Remark's Harbor House (707/642-8984), north on Harbor Way, offers seafood lunches (except Sunday) and dinners every day. The Szechuan Chef (707/643-1980), one of many Chinese restaurants, is at 2215 Sonoma Boulevard. City Lights Cafe (707/557-9200), downtown at 415 Virginia Street, is a fashionable weekday lunching spot that features California cuisine and homemade desserts.

At the eastern edge of the Benicia-Vallejo Highway (780) are turnoffs for **Glen Cove Marina**. Unless you have a boat berthed there, don't stop. Access to a minute section of shoreline is rough, and the imposing white building is for boat skippers who anchor here, although you might be allowed into the snack bar if it's open. Once a residence for keepers of the Carquinez Strait Lighthouse, this building was moved to the marina.

Benicia's Historic Sites and Shoreline Parks

The popular **Benicia State Recreation Area** (707/648-1911) between Vallejo and Benicia, off 780 and Columbus Parkway, is open from 8:00 A.M. to sunset. There's a small entrance fee to enjoy its 438 acres, although you can reach the parcourse from a small free parking lot near West K Street and Military West. Small saltwater marshes attract **birds** you don't often meet, like black rails and clapper rails. Several picnic areas have barbecue grills; there are restrooms, and drinking fountains that require deep bends to use. Besides a **parcourse**, there are enough trails to keep **hikers, joggers, and bicyclists** happy. One walking trail leading to Dillon Point has a wide view of the Carquinez bridge. A word of advice: If you're **fishing** or sitting on the sculptured rocks by the strait's edge, back up or you'll be drenched when a big ship or barge comes close.

Although **Benicia** calls itself historic with fervor, this town of around 20,000 people suffers from acute growing pains. The whine of bulldozers can be heard as suburban homes crawl over hillsides where sheep grazed not long ago. Yet much of the old way of life remains, and there are peaceful areas throughout this old town and along the revitalized portions of the waterfront.

Since 1847, when General Mariano Vallejo and Yankee partners started Benicia

Old Captain Walsh home in Benicia.

(named for Vallejo's wife), the town has had a seesaw of historic periods. Shortly after the first twenty or so adobe homes were built, most residents fled to hunt gold. When California became a state, Benicia offered its big, brick city hall as a state capitol. For just over a year, starting in 1853, the legislators met here; then they deserted to Sacramento.

During this period the U.S. Army established a huge arsenal, part of which burned in 1912. When the army removed the stored munitions in 1962, the town's population of 4,000, mostly soldiers and camp followers, dwindled. Artists, antique shop owners, and residents who liked life in a backwater moved in. Then came the developers. But all is not lost . . . yet.

To arrive at the official **historic downtown Benicia** from the west, take the Military West turnoff to First Street and turn right; from the East, turn left on East Fifth or Second streets and zig over to First Street. The kingpin is the **Benicia Capitol State Historic Park** (707/745-3385) at First and G Streets. The Capitol building looks like a capitol building should, with huge pillars and a wide staircase. Inside are restored chambers and offices, and exhibits from the short time in 1853 and 1854 when it was a working capitol. Next door, surrounding the home of Joseph Fischer, an early butcher, are serene, shadowed gardens.

Old homes like this are scattered throughout Benicia. Many are private, like the Captain Walsh home at 235 East L Street, which was shipped around the Horn in 1849 and reassembled. Weekdays you can get a map and a Historical Tour Guide at the **Chamber of Commerce** (707/745-2120) at 831 First Street.

Benicia is proud of its military past. Although more than 2,300 acres branching off from Military East are zoned as an industrial park, you can view several historic buildings, at least from the outside. The **guardhouse** on Grant Street near Adams Street is similar to an earlier one where Ulysses S. Grant, then a young lieutenant, was found guilty of firing a cannon across the Strait. (He was bored with duty here.) The **Post Cemetery** off Hospital Drive has gravestones dating from the mid 1840s. The 1859 **Clock Tower Fortress**, high on a hill in Johansen Square, once guarded the Strait; now it's a community center. Across the lawn the gracious 1860 **Commandant's Home**, presently a restaurant, overlooks a sea of imported Japanese cars at the Strait's edge.

To reach another cluster of history, starring the 1853–1854 **Camel Barns**, drive north on Park Road, continue under the freeway, and follow signs. In 1856 these handcrafted sandstone warehouses stabled a herd of camels that were to be used for desert transport. The camels proved unpopular. Besides their smell and nasty disposition, they made their riders seasick and frightened the horses. In 1864 they were auctioned off; in 1934 the last one died in a Los Angeles zoo. The Camel Barns now house the immaculate **Benicia Historical Museum** (707/745-5435), open Friday, Saturday, and Sunday afternoon.

A **free historic brochure** handed out by tourist-oriented enterprises calls First Street "the **Antiques Center** of the West." Among dozens of antique, clothing, and craft shops are those specializing in teddy bears, miniatures, glass, old toys, dolls, and almost anything you can think of. J. F. Tanner, at 615 First Street, is like an indoor flea market. Hagen's House of Clocks, 513 First, has the west's largest collection of clocks; try to visit on the hour, when they all start to chime and bong and cuckoo. Small, gifty businesses in the brick Tanner Building include a coffeehouse cum bookstore, a pastry company, and fine jewelry and photograph gallery. The Nantucket Fish Company Restaurant actually sells fish at its market next door.

The waterfront at the foot of First Street has awaited restoration for many a year. Even the ever-present ducks seem discouraged. Most of the bawdy houses where lonely soldiers once exchanged two dollars for t.l.c. have been razed. A plaque memorializing Jack London, who caroused nearby, is surrounded by litter, and the former Jurgensen's Saloon, where London did much of his drinking, is in a state of near collapse. The mustard yellow **transcontinental railroad depot** moved here at the turn of the century sits desolate in a weed-choked field; only rotting pilings remain from the 1879 Transcontinental Train Ferry Dock.

Now the **Point Benicia Pier** pokes out into the Strait within handshaking distance of passing ships and trains whistle mournfully by on the opposite shore. Optimists with fishing rods who bump out on the washboard road to the pier and brave the stiff breezes might catch sturgeon and striped bass.

For fancier ambience, note the luxury condominiums beyond the empty fields to the east. Some front on the small, pleasant **Benicia Marina** with its public walkways, benches, and snack bar. The marina's public parking lot is at the end of East B Street.

The scenic **Benicia Waterfront Pathway System** wends its way, with a few breaks, from the Marina to the east entrance of the Benicia State Recreation area. If you have time to stroll, hike, jog, or bike it—do. Otherwise drive along the edge, stopping at the various public access points and parks. If you can't locate an adequate map, just stay as close as you can to the water. You may get on some dead-end streets, but you'll also see some delightful parts of Benicia. Highlights are the quiet cove with stairways to the water at the end of West Third Street and the park between West Fourth and Fifth streets.

At the **Launching Ramp Park** at the foot of West Ninth Street, you'll find a small **fishing pier**, lots of wind, a cafe where you can quaff beer or play pool with locals, and a public restroom. The monument at the point is dedicated to Commodore Jones, the historic figure who briefly took over Monterey before war was officially declared with Mexico.

The **Twelfth and K Shoreline Park**, directly across the Strait from Port Costa, is a stunner. You can sit in your car to enjoy the views or join local ducks and picnic outside. Hopefully, the restroom will be built by the time you arrive. There's another **charming park**, this one a walk-in, at West Thirteenth and K Streets. If you continue on past the tiny West Fourteenth Street Park, you'll notice an adobe building on L Street, surrounded by roses, a gazebo, duck decoys, and a plethora of odd adornments. This is The Adobe, a private halfway house. Continue east, and you'll soon be at the Benicia State Recreation area again.

Where to eat? At Sam's Harbor (707/745-9962), 710 West I Street, you can lunch or dine inside or outside on the deck right on the water. This is a favorite gathering spot for local citizens, ducks, and children; geese sometimes lay eggs in the window boxes. Easy-to-find restaurants along First Street include the Union Hotel (707/746-0100), Washington House Deli Cafe for breakfast and lunch, First Street Foods (707/745-4404), and the Nantucket Fish Company (707/745-2233). Hours vary, but one of these places is sure to be open when you need nourishment. The Commandant's Residence (707/745-6880) mentioned earlier is for quiet, leisurely dining; reservations are recommended.

Where to stay? The historic pamphlet lists the Benicia Inn (707/745-9901) at 150 West J Street. The Union Hotel (707/746-0100) at 401 First Street offers twelve rooms dressed up with antiques and jacuzzis. Captain Dillingham's Inn (707/746-7164) at 145 East D Street features decks and patios plus ten renovated rooms with jacuzzis.

San Quentin Point and Edge of Larkspur

Where do locals go for Bayside recreation, you might wonder as you drive Highway 101 through the East Marin mixture of shopping malls and industries? But small to big retreats do exist, some hidden away, where you can **canoe, swim, fish, bird, hike and bike**, or just relax. They're all there, waiting discovery.

If you arrive from the East Bay on the hunchback **Richmond–San Rafael Bridge**, the Bay is framed to the north by Point San Pedro and on the south by the Tiburon Peninsula and Point San Quentin (named after the renegade Indian, Quentin). Marin's favorite, Mount Tamalpais (which some say resembles an Indian maiden) is there, always an impressive backdrop. No wonder a child was overheard calling it "Templepais."

The long dock just north of the Richmond–San Rafael Bridge approach belongs to the private Marin Rod and Gun Club and is off limits to the public. You're welcome, however to tour San Quentin—the small town, that is—not **San Quentin Prison**. For this quick detour, take the turnoff nearest the Richmond–San Rafael Bridge and follow signs. You can drive down Main Street past deserted buildings and homes for prison personnel to a post office where you can have your mail postmarked "San Quentin" to surprise friends and relatives. But ask the man to hand cancel it for you. There's also a small gift shop just outside the prison gate, but the selection is limited; the guard at the gate will get someone to open it for you. That's all, but where else, unless you commit an adequate crime, can you get so close to a famous prison?

The dusty, decrepit 1924 Hutchinson Quarry on Sir Francis Drake Boulevard is gone, and only the tall chimney and brick ovens remain from the Remillard Brickyard, whose bricks helped rebuild San Francisco after the 1906 quake and fire. What stands out now is an airy modern structure of white pipes in the shape of an inverted triangle—the **Larkspur Ferry Terminal**. Its design is eye-catching, but passengers sometimes have to huddle in a tiny glassed-in area to escape wind, fog, and rain.

You pay less than for most regular Bay cruises to board this comfortable gas-turbine ferry for a trip between San Francisco and Larkspur. You can buy coffee, donuts, hot dogs, snacks, or cocktails in the passenger's lounge; outside there's plenty of deck space to commune with seagulls and pelicans. Call Golden Gate Transit (San Francisco, 415/332-6600; Marin, 415/453-2100) for times and fares.

If you park at the terminal lot and walk to the edge of **Corte Madera Creek**, you may surprise a lone great egret or a flock of birds that has strayed over from the ninety-five-acre **Corte Madera Marsh Ecological Reserve**. Residents of the Greenbrae Boardwalk arks, i.e., houseboats, also on the opposite shore, are more intimate with this winged wildlife. On **Muzzi Marsh** adjoining the preserve, be sure you stay on the levee; walking anywhere else might destroy the delicate ecological balance.

As a contrast to the open marshes, across Sir Francis Drake Boulevard is **Larkspur Landing**—acres of tastefully designed offices and housing, and more than fifty restaurants and shops. You can walk or bike over on the overpass to check out the array of gifts, books, art, fashions, groceries, or whatever you need. As for restaurants, you can eat: Mexican—Acapulco (415/461-8044); Mandarin Chinese—Yet Wah (415/461-3631); Japanese—Sushi Ko (415/461-8400); Italian seafood—Scoma's (415/461-6161); natural food—Good Earth (415/461-7322); American in a dining room or on a patio—Henderson's Grandmother (415/461-5800); or contemporary European with greenery—Baxter's (415/461-7022).

Along Corte Madera Creek

If visiting a shopping center isn't your idea of fun, roam the **Cross-Marin bicycle (and hiking) trail** along Corte Madera Creek, as it wanders east through the well-endowed towns of Corte Madera and Larkspur. You can pick up the trail on Sir

San Quentin Prison. In town you can visit the gift shop and post office.

Francis Drake Boulevard outside the ferry terminal; it's flat and well paved enough for **wheelchairs**.

Just before the trail ducks under the first Highway 101 overpass is a simulated old western town, reported to be made of lumber from the late Hutchinson Quarry. The most visible occupant, Growing Concern, sells antiques and reproductions of antiques. Where the town's fake street ends on the creek you'll glimpse an old drawbridge that used to open for boats before the higher tangle of highway overpasses was built.

As you follow the trail along the sunny, north side of Corte Madera Creek, fancy industrial buildings, some half built, are to the north. Across the creek you glimpse many-decked mansions, most with a yacht or big boat tied to a private dock. On the creek itself, grebes and other waterfowl paddle about and dive for food. You can pause to savor these scenes at benches and picnic tables scattered en route. There's even a tree or two. The creekside path ends at South Eliseo Drive, but you can continue on city sidewalks and streets past clusters of apartment complexes by other creekside parks to the big **Corte Madera Creekside Park**.

Bon Air Landing Park, a morsel of serenity, is popular with ducks and gulls. Farther west, **Hamilton Park**, northeast of the Bon Air Bridge, is a hangout for geese that panhandle from nearby office and medical workers. Clarabelle Hamilton, who resided in a neighboring retirement home, donated this lot so that people would have "lasting access to the creek."

If you prefer transporting yourself on four wheels, find your way to Lucky Drive along the south edge of Corte Madera Creek (take the overpass if you're walking or biking). Lining the creek is a string of arks, some built as vacation homes in the early 1900s, others more recently. Another collection, along Larkspur Boardwalk, backs up to Piper Park.

Piper Park, a forty-acre oasis of grass on Doherty, which branches off Lucky Drive, is a great place to play team sports. Or you can stroll to the park's small pier to admire ducks, forested Marin mountains, plush homes, and highrise apartments on the lagoons and hills. **Cricket anyone?** Piper Park also boats a cricket field. On many weekends white-clad members of the fifty-year old Marin Cricket Club play this oddball game. One participant described it as a "cross between baseball and a long afternoon nap." Perhaps the game's most unusual aspect is that it's bad taste to disagree with the umpire.

Marin residents—and you—can enjoy other water-oriented parks. Continue west and cross the creek on Bon Air Road. Near the Marin General Hospital is the twenty-six-acre **Corte Madera Creek Park**, which is actually in Larkspur, Greenbrae, and Kentfield. It includes a **hiking and jogging trail** and a restored saltwater **marsh**.

The San Rafael Canal

Along **San Rafael Canal** to the north parks are rare, but the restaurant and boating action can be interesting. From Highway 101 take the Central San Rafael exit, go east on Second Street, and right on Grand Street to Francisco Boulevard.

To reach **Pickleweed Park**, 50 Canal, turn left on Harbor Street from Francisco Boulevard and drive to the mouth of the canal. This six acres of turfed fill contains an active community center, a **parcourse Fitness Circuit**, and a glimpse of the Bay from the levee. Blink and you'll miss wee, adjoining **Schoen Park**, popular with children because of its playground. Another tiny **Beach Park** is inland on Beach Park Road off Francisco Boulevard.

The **San Rafael Yacht Club and Harbor** fronts on the narrow canal. So does the casual, publike Pier 15 Restaurant on 15 Harbor Street (415/453-9978), where you can dine overlooking water after you hitch your boat to the restaurant's dock. Dominic's Harbor Restaurant (415/456-1383) at 507 Francisco Boulevard, which advertises seafood from "our own family boats," also has a boat dock and outside deck plus acres of parking.

Around Point San Pedro to McNear's Beach and China Camp

Whether you're driving or pedaling, you can escape crowded concrete on a surprisingly isolated **nine-mile driving or biking shoreline loop** that has moments of great beauty. Follow the Point San Pedro Road that starts on the north side of the canal near the Central San Rafael exit off Highway 101. Turn east on Second Street, which eases into Third, which in turn becomes Point San Pedro Road.

At first you drive through suburban sprawl, then you pass two small yacht harbors. Farther along, south on Loch Lomond Drive, is the larger **Loch Lomond Marina**. There you'll find bait, beer, food, a charter fishing boat, and a yacht club.

Off the Loch Lomond Marina you can see **West Marin and East Marin Islands** not far off shore. At last report, this pair of private islands was for sale. If you've ever yearned to own your own island and have several million dollars to spare, this is your chance. The old Crowley Tugboat Company bought the pair at auction in 1926 for $25,438. On ten-acre East Marin Island, Crowley planted date palms and other exotic trees and erected two stone guesthouses. William Randolph Hearst once owned the caretaker's ark, which he used for floating poker games.

Two-and-a-half-acre West Marin Island was never developed. The Audubon Society would like to see this small secluded island preserved for the snowy egrets and black-crowned night herons that nest here, but the multimillion dollar price tag is a deterrent. Sorry, both islands display big "no trespassing" signs.

Back to San Pedro Point Road, the peaceful "country" portion of the nine-mile loop starts soon after you pass a Bay-edge **hiking trail**. If you're a golfer, there's the eighteen-hole **Peacock Gap Golf and Country Club**. Follows signs on Riviera to its 128 scenic acres and lagoon plus a clubhouse with restaurant and bar (415/453-4122) at 333 Biscayne Drive. If you miss the Riviera turnoff, turn west at Biscayne Drive a mile farther.

McNear's Beach County Park

Shortly after you pass the entrance to the venerable McNear's Brickyard (you'll see its tall smokestacks), watch for Cantera Way, which leads to the fifty-two acre **McNear's Beach County Park**. No wonder generations have made pilgrimages here. It's sheltered, usually sunny, and one of the rare parks where you can **swim in both the Bay or a pool**. Besides these assets, there's a **beach, tennis courts, grassy**

picnic and lounging area, and snack bar. There's also an entrance fee, upped on weekends and holidays.

China Camp State Park

A few turns later, after you climb back up to San Pedro Point Road, you enter **China Camp State Park** (415/456-0766), 1,648 acres of the most completely natural watershed remaining along the shores of San Francisco Bay. Even if you just drive through, the roadside overlooks are worth it.

As for recreation, you can **wade, swim, bird watch, sunbathe, and fish**. When the tide is high enough—especially in winter and spring—anglers bring in striped bass, flounder, silver and rubberlip perch, and an occasional sturgeon.

Historic **China Camp Village** has been painted and photographed for decades; also the classic 1954 movie, *Blood Alley*, starring John Wayne and Lauren Bacall, was shot in the area. The camp was settled in the 1860s by Chinese after the gold mines played out and the transcontinental railroad was built. Soon nearly 500 villagers were involved in fishing, mainly for shrimp, which they dried on the hillside and shipped back to China. But when national employment slumped, anti-Chinese sentiment rose. Fishing limitations were set, and in 1905, export of dried shrimp was banned. Only a few Chinese fishermen, using new methods, managed to hang on. That they did was providential, for thousands of Chinese found refuge here in camps or shacks over the water after the 1906 San Francisco earthquake and fire.

A second exodus began when a 1913 fire destroyed most of the shanties. As the years went by, the once-bustling village was reduced to a rickety dock, a line of rotting boats, and a few ramshackle buildings. You can see remnants of foundations of long-gone homes and shops and perhaps uncover a Chinese artifact in the orchard picnic area to the south or the **Rat Rock Cove Beach** to the north. After they were given this thirty-six-acre village in 1977 by Chinn Ho, a Hawaiian developer, state park people repaired roofs and painstakingly restored the buildings and dock to look as they had for so many decades.

Frank Quan, a descendant of original settlers, still lives at China Camp. He operates a fishing business and sells most of his catch as bait. But ask at the snack bar (usually open weekends) if he has brought in any fresh grass shrimp; it's steamed right there at the pier in an old-fashioned brick-based oven: some consider it the best eating shrimp in the world.

Among other treats, you can visit the small museum if it's open, where photographs and memorabilia recall the busy shrimping period. A few picnic tables sit on the beach edge here. For more panoramic overlooks, you can picnic at China Camp Point, just above the village, or Five Pines Point. In addition, Weber and Buckeye points, farther north, have barbecues. The park's extensive marshes and mudflats attract many **birds**. **Hobie Cat sailors** come here and so do campers. The **Back Ranch Campground** at the park's north edge has thirty-eight walk-in sites; call 415/456-1286. Warning—be sure your camera is loaded with film, particularly when spring wildflowers cover the hillsides.

After you leave the park, you can continue on through residential Santa Venetia, which an optimistic developer hoped to turn into a creekside Venice, Italy. Eventually you'll arrive at the back of the Marin Civic Center.

Three Small Open Space Sanctuaries

En route, take time to enjoy three lesser known stops, little gems of natural beauty in the **Marin County Open Space District**. This Marin organization was established in 1972 by general election to "preserve and protect the natural environment in strategic open spaces and to provide an undisturbed habitat for native plants and animals."

You reach the first open space preserve by taking the Vendola Drive turnoff to **Santa Venetia Marsh** outside the park boundary on Point San Pedro Road. In spring when tides and the fresh water of Gallinas Creek feed this high marsh, it's a blaze of brass buttons. But all year you'll meet a variety of **birds** on the outer levee walk.

Back to Point San Pedro Road, about a mile after the marsh turnoff, opposite a 7–11 convenience store, take Meadow Drive on your right to another open space find, **Santa Margarita Island**. Park and walk across the tiny bridge to this small enchanted woodland in the south fork of Gallinas Creek. A short trail circles the island and another leads up the hill through the dramatic rocks and native oaks (also be wary of poison oak).

Hiking trails lead to the upper reaches of sizable **San Pedro Mountain Preserve**, where you have superb views of both the Bay and the golden spire and blue roof of the Marin Civic Center. To reach this preserve, take the short Woodoaks Drive east shortly after the turnoff to Santa Margarita Island.

Frank Lloyd Wright's Controversial Marin Civic Center

The **Marin Civic Center**, with its series of graceful arches and dome, was designed so that one building would organically span the valleys between three hills. To decide how you rate this last commission of Frank Lloyd Wright, try to join a volunteer-led tour by calling 415/499-6104.

If no guide is available, at least visit the Administration Building with its balconies and curved glass skylight that allows tropical and semitropical plants to flourish on the ground floor. The top floor cafeteria, open to the public, has modest prices. You can eat inside or outside around a fountain on the tranquil eastern portion.

The grounds, too, are memorable. When you leave the building and stroll through the lovely area around the lagoon, you almost forget the noise and traffic on Highway 101. For an overall picture of Marin beyond the busy highway or of the Civic Center itself, climb the small grass-covered hill to the west.

Little-Known John F. McInnis Park

Four-hundred-fifty-acre **John F. McInnis Park**, on the north side of Gallinas Creek, is also within viewing distance of Frank Lloyd Wright's masterpiece. To reach the park, take the Smith Ranch Road exit off Highway 101 to the east. From the Civic Center, it's less nerve-wracking to take the Civic Center Drive frontage road north (notice the Duck Crossing signs) and turn right on Smith Ranch Road at the busy **Northgate Shopping Center**.

McInnis Park is relatively new and, thus, a bit raw looking, but it has a **canoe**

launching pier and you can look across the creek at sheep grazing and small planes landing. The park also has **playing fields, tennis courts, and an equestrian area**. It's also dog-walking country.

Where to eat? Besides the Marin Civic Center cafeteria, nearby restaurants include The Grotto of Marin (415/472-4070), 3751 Redwood Highway, for seafood and Taverna Yiasou (415/479-2991), 48 North San Pedro Road, for Greek dinners. Or join hungry locals at the friendly Le Chalet Basque (415/479-1070), 405 North San Pedro Road a mile east of Civic Center, where you can eat inside on checked tablecloths or outside on the deck. In a hurry? You'll find fast-food stops at or near the Northgate Mall. Restaurants here include the Hungry House (415/472-4020), the Royal Mandarin (415/472-5676), and Roast Haus II (415/472-2233). Also, along downtown San Rafael's Fourth Street, you can eat your way around the world.

Frank Lloyd Wright's Marin Civic Center: a controversial masterpiece.

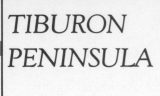

TIBURON PENINSULA

Arriving at the Promised Land

Soon after you leave Vista Point north of the Golden Gate Bridge, Highway 101 burrows into Marin coastal cliffs and hills through the **Waldo Tunnel**. Above the tunnel's entrance is a rainbow, painted—according to legend—by a mysterious night-time artist, perhaps a moonlighting member of the Highway Department. A local artist is raising money to tile the rainbow so it will stay eternally bright.

Once past the rainbow you enter a portion of golden Marin extolled by naturalists, yachtsmen, birders, bicyclists, hikers, artists, real estate agents, and fervid inhabitants (not all of whom own hot tubs). When you take the **Tiburon Boulevard** turnoff off Highway 101, you'll know why this real estate is so coveted. In spite of new housing crowding the hills, there's still green open space close by the Bay; in the distance San Francisco shimmers at each turn.

Tiburon Wildlife Refuge and a Shoreline Park

For a peaceful interlude and a chance to meet many of Marin's birds, plants, and trees, visit the **Richardson Bay Wildlife Sanctuary**, open Wednesday through Sunday, with guided walks on Sunday. Turn right off Tiburon Boulevard near the Tiburon border and drive to 376 Greenwood Beach Road. Park along the fence and walk down past a rusty metal pelican to the **Audubon Society's Center** (415/388-2524), which contains a bookstore and small museum. If the naturalist and volunteers on duty remember, they'll collect a tiny admission fee; if you're an Audubon Society member, you're in free.

The society acquired this eleven acres of moderately dry land and nine-hundred acres of shallow, muddy Bay land in order to feed and protect local birds and the **hundreds of thousands of waterfowl and shorebirds** on their flyway from October through March.

At first as you look out over the Bay, the western grebes, ruddy ducks, and less common birds may look like dots of pepper sprinkled on the water. Then something frightens them. Perhaps a harbor seal surfaces. As the birds swirl by, you begin to comprehend their sheer numbers. You may see nine varieties of gulls, egrets, great blue herons, common wading birds by the dozen, plus greater and lesser scaups, surf scoters, rare black scoters, and Barrow's goldeneyes.

You can watch this water and air show—with San Francisco far off on a silvery blue-green platter—from atop a tiny hill on a self-guided **nature trail**. Or you can sit on an ornate white cast iron chair on the veranda of Marin's oldest Victorian, the beautifully restored 1876 **Lyford house**, which was barged over from Strawberry Point in 1957. Guided tours of the interior are often given on Sunday afternoons. You'll learn that Dr. Benjamin F. Lyford, an embalming surgeon and pioneer in making corpses look lifelike (he kept his embalming chemicals in the tower), married Hilarita Reed, a descendant of an early Mexican land grantee.

If you visit the Audubon refuge on a weekday, you might glimpse naturalist Elizabeth Terwilliger helping a group of school children discover the *Sights and Sounds of the Season*, the title of her popular book, as she has done for decades. Nature trips led by the fabled "Mrs. T" are so popular, a foundation in her name (415/454-6965) now handles reservations and also her film series "Tripping with Terwilliger," which is shown to millions of school children every year.

After you leave the sanctuary and drive east past **Blackie's Pasture**, an open field where the old swaybacked horse spent his declining years, you can join residents out walking pedigreed dogs, jogging, or otherwise benefiting from well-groomed **Shoreline Park**. There are slides for the preschool set, rocks for kids to clamber over, and benches for all ages to sit on as they gaze at that view. This oasis hugs the water until you reach the miniscule downtown of **Tiburon**.

Tiburon and Belvedere

You're already in Tiburon, of course, if you've arrived by ferry. This may be a good idea, as parking can be tight, especially on weekends. Including a stop in Sausalito, the Red & White Fleet's catamaran **ferry** takes thirty-five minutes from San Francisco but zips back in fifteen minutes; call 415/546-2815 for fare and schedules.

Tiburon's Main Street shops and dockside watering holes are worth investigating. At Sam's Anchor Cafe (415/435-4527)—as generations have done—you can drink beer or dine on the deck, watched by seagulls while you watch ferries come and go to San Francisco or Angel Island. But Sam's, the Dock, and other restaurants with bayside decks are often crowded, so leave your name and browse the shops during the hour or two wait. Or pick up a quick, tasty morsel at the Sweden House Bakery. If you run out of Main Street shops, **Ark Row** has two levels more. These turn-of-the-century houseboat-arks—now landlocked—contain boutiques; delis (try Michael's Cafe); a bike shop; antique and craft shops; and Tiburon Vintners, at 72 Main Street, which offers **wine tasting** of their more than thirty varieties.

For a high-level outlook, climb the stairs to **Corinthian Island** by the big, white Corinthian Yacht Club near Belvedere's border. Was it originally an island or a peninsula? For thirty years, starting in 1855, Israel Kashow, an irascible giant, squatted on Belvedere with his large family. When the government came to take over the Bay islands, Kashow led officials over a spit at low tide, convincing them it was a peninsula. Kashow could not convince the courts, however, that he had a legal right to this piece of land. It belonged to heirs of **John Thomas Reed**, who received a grant in 1831 to occupy the 8,878-acre **Rancho Corte de Madera del Presidio**, including all of the Tiburon Peninsula to Mill Valley and parts of Larkspur and Corte Madera.

How did Irishman Reed come by all this? In 1826, at the age of twenty-one, he reached California on his uncle's ship. Since Reed was Catholic and spoke fluent Spanish, he easily became a naturalized Mexican citizen and eventually received this huge land grant. Reed wasn't lucky for long, though. He died only eight years after marrying Hilaria Sanchez, daughter of the commander of the San Francisco Presidio. Friends bled him to cure his sunstroke and couldn't stem the flow of blood.

For a high caliber sampling of this former grant, loop up and around hilly, prestigious **Belvedere**, perhaps pausing at the town's tiny lagoon-park on Leeward. Take San Rafael Avenue to West Shore Road to Belvedere Avenue, and on up short Pine to Golden Gate Avenue, where you can stroll on Pomander Walk, a tree-shaded lane near the crest of the hill. As you pass the luxurious homes, each with a sweeping view, many with a private dock, it's hard not to be jealous. Return on Pine to Belvedere Avenue to Beach Road and continue back past the San Francisco Yacht Club.

Another viewing point is near **Old St. Hilary's in the Wildflowers**, a tiny "carpenter gothic" church, built circa 1886, high on the hill above Tiburon. Call the Landmarks Society at 415/435-1853 for times the church is open. This Historic Preserve is worth the trip up to admire the 217 species of ferns, sedges, rushes, wildflowers, and other plants, many uncommon, some that grow only here.

Just east of the ferry landing on Tiburon Boulevard a new green **shoreline park**

Diners have been enjoying the atmosphere at Sam's in Tiburon for generations.

has sprouted in front of the massive Point Tiburon development. Plans call for 23,000 square feet of shops and restaurants to be added to those already in this tiny town. A popular local bumper sticker reads, "I survived Tiburon Boulevard." Now that Point Tiburon has arrived, the boulevard is again viable.

At the eastern end of the park, near the Caprice Restaurant (reservations suggested; call 415/435-3400), Tiburon Boulevard becomes **Paradise Drive**. Wedged among the apartments hanging out over the Bay is **Elephant Rock**, where only those sixteen years and under can **fish**, although older visitors are allowed on this minipier wrapped around a rock. The name Tiburon means *shark*, but more likely catches are perch, rockfish, and even striped bass.

A short distance farther is the **Stone Tower**, built about 1889 by Dr. Lyford, mentioned earlier, as a gateway to his "Hygeia," which he hoped to fill with healthful-living teetotalers. The tower is all that's left of his Utopian dream.

Where to stay in Tiburon? The popular Tiburon Lodge (415/435-3133), 1651 Tiburon Boulevard, is it. Rooms look out over the hills, Point Tiburon condos, or the pool and patio.

Paradise Drive and Ring Mountain Preserve

If admiring Tiburon and Belvedere estates and yachts is too rich a diet, you'll find open areas of natural beauty ahead. Continue one twisty mile on Paradise Drive and park across from the National Marine Fisheries entrance gate. You'll see the start of the steep trail that winds up through bay trees, oak, and ferns in the **Tiburon Uplands County Park**.

For a more manicured park, stay on Paradise Drive to **Paradise Beach County Park**. You can also reach it by turning left on Trestle Glen Boulevard off Tiburon Boulevard soon after you leave Highway 101. Here, for a parking fee, you can get in on many varieties of waterfront recreation. You can sunbathe or doze on grass that slopes down to the water. There's a **wading beach** for kids, a pier for fisherfolk, and picnic facilities include charcoal grills. More good news: Because this is the leeward side of the peninsula, the weather is usually balmy and the water warm enough for swimming—well, usually. Arrive early on summer weekends and holidays. This park has been popular with decades of sun worshippers.

The enchanted **Ring Mountain Preserve**, 377 acres patrolled by hawks, is a highlight of the Tiburon Peninsula. Take the Paradise Drive exit off Highway 101 and drive one-and-three-fourths miles. Look for the wooden entry sign and bridge to your right opposite a marsh (across Corte Madera Channel from San Quentin State Prison). Treat yourself to several hours to investigate this magical kingdom that rises to a height of 600 feet. In the spring and early summer wildflowers paint the slopes in many colors; often a resident meadowlark presents a free concert.

Part of Ring Mountain's magic is that you can see a portion of California the way it was thousands of years ago. Wind still rustles native grasses on the lower open slopes; they have not been bulldozed away or driven out by introduced species. On the upper slopes and ridges, greenish jadelike serpentine, from small boulders to huge monoliths, thrust out from the earth. In the thin, gravelly soil, away from the competition below, rare and endangered plants and flowers like the Tiburon paintbrush, the Marin dwarf flax, and the Tiburon mariposa lily can cope.

During winter through early summer, ribbons of water course and trickle down the mountainside; later seeps and springs provide water for the flowers, plants, and canopies of dark green bay and live oak trees. In these miniature forests are circles of seclusion where you might meet a native gray fox, deer, or quail while jays scold you.

Ring Mountain, which acquired its name at the turn of the century from a neighboring supervisor, has centuries of history going for it. Near the ridge is a huge rock with circular petroglyphs chiseled by unknown native Americans perhaps 2,000 years ago. In the early 1800s the mountain was part of Reed's land grant, and his cattle grazed here. For nearly 150 years it remained, undeveloped, in the hands of this pioneer family. The one exception was a military installation at the top. Few signs of its intrusion remain. Nature is taking back its own; flowers now poke up through crumbling asphalt and concrete.

That this mountain has remained much as it was before the Whiteskins arrived is due to the concern of conservation-minded citizens who realized its biological, archaeological, and geological value. The **Nature Conservancy**, a nonprofit organization devoted to acquiring and managing ecologically significant land, played a key role. The Nature Conservancy now owns or manages 377 crucial acres of Ring Mountain. At 10 A.M. on most Sundays, volunteers lead guests along the well-maintained trails and point out the many rare plants and flowers. Call the Nature Conservancy at 415/777-0487 or the Ring Mountain Preserve at 415/927-1230 to verify dates.

On Ring Mountain wherever you look is beautiful. The mudflats below display upside down reflections of the mountains ringing the Bay. Even the rocks are alive with the grays, greens, and rusts of lichen. Frequently small lizards skitter by or stand, quivering, until you pass. On all sides the sea of grass ripples with wide bands of green or burnished yellows and reds. Occasionally the shadow of a hawk passes over.

Once you reach the ridge top, crowned by Turtle Rock, Mount Tamalpais rises to the west and the city of St. Francis appears to the southeast, sometimes only the tips of its buildings floating above the fog. You can also see the Bay Bridge, the San Rafael Bridge, and a hint of the Golden Gate Bridge.

Because its beauty has been preserved, Ring Mountain can be enjoyed by future generations as well as children. School groups often visit. On one such day a hiker stepped aside to let a group of small boys on a nature expedition pass.

One boy looked up at the hiker, his face full of awe, "Do you own this place?"

"Oh, no," the woman replied, "I think God owns it."

The boy nodded in agreement.

ANGEL ISLAND STATE PARK

Getting Away in the Middle of the Bay

On the feast day of Nuestra Señora de los Angeles in August 1775, Coast Miwok Indians in tule boats cautiously watched Lt. Don Juan Mañuel de Ayala's tiny packet *San Carlos* anchor in a secluded cove off a large, heavily wooded island. Although Sir Francis Drake may have dropped by in 1579, Ayala's was the first documented European ship to enter San Francisco Bay. Ayala admired the cove's beautiful harmony and stayed on for several weeks while his men charted the Bay for Spain.

Why had it taken so long? Why, as shell mounds indicate, had the Indians lived or camped along the edges of this great natural harbor, undisturbed, for as long as 5,000 years? Historians believe that it was the location of this, the Bay's largest island, plus fog, that hid the Bay's narrow entrance from the ships of exploring Whiteskins.

Now, because environmentalist Caroline Livermore and others helped preserve these 740 acres as an island-park, inaccessible to visitor's cars, you can savor much of the quiet harmony that the Miwoks and Ayala enjoyed.

In the relatively few centuries since its discovery, **Angel Island** has known unharmonious periods. The island now has enough magnificent stands of trees to qualify it as a wilderness, yet it was once denuded of forests. In *Two Years Before the Mast*, Richard Henry Dana recalled how he and fellow sailors were sent here to cut wood. Other seafaring men reported seeing ghosts walking on the moonlit paths and there were rumors of smugglers and pirates. In 1839 the Mexican government allowed Antonio Maria Osio to graze sheep and cattle, which didn't help the island's native plant life. Then, in 1850, the U.S. Army took over. You can relive the next century of military history.

But first drop into the **Ayala Cove Visitor Center** (415/435-1915). It's behind a huge waving flag a short walk from the ferry dock. A 50 cent map and brochure and the free displays here give you a quick overview of the island and its past. You learn Ayala Cove was once called Hospital Cove because of a quarantine station where immigrants, travelers, and seamen were isolated to wait out the incubation time of infectious tropical diseases.

For a real overview, those hardy enough can hike up to **Mount Livermore's 781-foot summit**. Whateve trail you take, avoid **poison oak** or you may endure days of itching misery. The Sunset Trail starts from the west side of Ayala Cove. Steps go steeply up from near the ferry dock to the North Ridge Trail which clambers up and up through shadowed trees and open meadows thick with flowers. Exotics like the purple of tower of jewels or pride of Madeira were brought to the island from as far away as the Canary Islands and the East Indies, and **spring wildflowers by the thousands** are here because tons of seeds, donated by a San Francisco garden club, were sown from the air.

You will also see land and sea birds and, in uncrowded areas, perhaps deer. The original black-tail deer may have swum across deep Raccoon Strait from Marin: Early visitors reported seeing "seals with horns" making the trip. When these were hunted to extinction, mule deer were imported; there has been much controversy as to how to handle the overgrazing of present herds. The resident raccoons? They may have swum over or hitched a ride on driftwood.

On either trail, or on the easier-to-walk Fire Road Trail that also winds to the top, the higher you climb, the deeper the quiet, the fresher the breeze, and the more magnificent the views. At the summit, from the paved heliport and **picnic area** (with restrooms), you have a world-caliber **360-degree panorama**. When you can tear yourself away, walk down the Sunset Trail to the paved, six-mile long **hiking, biking, and wheelchair-accessible Perimeter Trail** that circles the island. Of course, you can also connect with this trail from Ayala Cove. Just follow signs.

If you hike or bike towards the western shore, you can experience a taste of Civil War days at **Camp Reynolds (West Garrison)**. The army started this once busy post

Protected Ayala Cove on Angel Island is the perfect lunchtime spot for day sailors.

in 1863. The parade ground, brick quartermaster's warehouse, old bakehouse, and some ten officer's homes survive. One beautifully restored home, Quarters #11, is open to the public, usually from noon to three on weekends. At times, when special groups are there, docents dressed in period costumes bake bread in the restored brick oven, or sing and dance to music from an 1880 pump organ; on weekends they may help visitors shoot a twelve-pound mountain howitzer. Ask the Angel Island Association docents (415/435-3522) or at the Ayala Cove Visitor's Center for times.

If you're not into military history, put on your windbreaker for the short detour on a dirt road to **Point Stuart** on the island's most westerly tip, where you'll find a warning bell and light and more dramatic views of San Francisco and across Raccoon Strait to Marin County.

Continuing southeast, a spur path leads to **Perles Beach** where you can **picnic** and **sunbathe**. The water is cold and choppy, but beachcombing can be great and there's always that view. You can also investigate more military remnants near the Perimeter Road: **Battery Wallace, Battery Ledyard**, and **Battery Drew**. These Endicott batteries, built in 1898 during the Spanish-American War, were outdated shortly after completion. (So was the off limits Nike Missile launching site farther east, obsolete seven years after was established in 1955.)

At the island's windy—note the windmill—southeast corner is **Point Blunt** with a working lighthouse and foghorn. It's off limits to the public, but not to barking sea lions who haul out here. Offshore parades of sailboats take advantage of the stiff breezes. Around the corner on the leeward side, some of them run out of breeze; you can hear their flapping sails far away.

Now you're on the eastern side of the island, coming up to **Fort McDowell (East Garrison)**. Ahead are the ghostly remains of buildings where hundreds of thousands of American troops were "processed" for the Spanish-American and Second World wars and where those lucky enough to return were deactivated. The huge concrete structure was once a barracks holding 600 men. Although the tidy little chapel has been restored, most other buildings are crumbling away and are unsafe to enter.

Near East Garrison are numerous facilities for small and group **picnics**. Sandy **Quarry Beach** is great for **sunbathing**, but swimming is not recommended anywhere around the island. The water is too cold, the currents and tides too swift, and there are no lifeguards (who might have trouble themselves).

You can hike on for fifteen minutes to Ayala Cove, or turn off shortly at a wooded path down to **North Garrison** and the **Immigration Station**. At the end, fringed by palm trees, is pleasant, sandy **Winslow Cove** with picnic tables overlooking the water. What makes this serene scene different? In the center of a grassy lawn is a monument with Chinese calligraphy: "Leaving their homes and villages, they crossed the ocean only to endure confinement in these barracks. Conquering frontiers and barriers, they pioneered a new life by the Golden Gate."

"Trader Vic" Bergeron erected this monument in 1979 to commemorate the ordeal of Chinese immigrants here, especially during the Chinese Exclusion Acts of 1882 to 1943. Although the cove had been used first by Indians, then Chinese shrimp fishermen, and later to detain World War II Japanese and German POWs, its most notorious function was as the "Ellis Island of the West" from 1910 to 1940.

Many immigrants, including several hundred Japanese picture brides, were inmates, but the Chinese detainees probably numbered 50,000. The 1906 earthquake and fire had destroyed most records verifying citizenship through the father, so some bought papers identifying them as the children of American citizens. During this period of anti-Asian sentiment, the Bureau of Immigration grilled the detainees to verify their claim.

You can visit one of the cramped, dingy barracks where the arrivals were kept for weeks, even years, before questioning. Ninety bunks three tiers high in the women's section, and 200 bunks in the men's offer a mute tribute to these immigrants. A knowledgeable ranger is on duty weekends to describe this sad chapter of history. Its record is in the poetry, now covered by layers of paint, telling of frustration and anguish. One inmate carved: "Even if it is built of jade, it is turned into a cage." Another:

> The floating clouds, the fog darken the sky.
> The moon shines faintly as the insects chirp.
> Grief and bitterness entwined are heaven sent.
> The sad person sits alone, leaning by a window.

When you return to Ayala Cove, you can join the many visitors who have stayed at the picnic grounds—and missed enjoying the rest of this beautiful island. You can also recuperate at the small **snack bar** near the ferry dock.

Red & White ferries (415/546-2815) run from Pier 43½ in San Francisco seven days a week during the summer, leaving there at 10 A.M. and 2 P.M. Weekends and holidays the schedule is increased. A limited number of bicycles are accepted on a first-come basis. The less-expensive Angel Island ferries (415/435-2131) leave from Tiburon hourly (not always on time) every day from 10 A.M. to 5 P.M. during the summer. They charge a slight extra fee for bikes. **Private boats** are welcome to use the mooring buoys at Ayala Cove or Quarry Beach and can stay overnight. They can also use the boat slips at Ayala Cove when the park is open from 8 A.M. to sunset. There's a small fee for either choice.

Overnight campers who don't mind fog, blasting foghorns, and aggressive raccoons can stay in one of the walk-in environmental **campgrounds** by reserving far in advance. Call 1-800-952-5580 for camping information. For information on Angel Island Park itself, phone 415/435-1915 or 415/435-3522.

MARIN
SOUTH
NEAR *the*
GOLDEN
GATE
BRIDGE

South Edge of Golden Marin

If you're headed for Marin on a crisp, clear day, especially with out-of-town guests and rolls of color film, treat everyone to a stop at Vista Point just north of the Golden Gate Bridge.

For an even more spectacular panorama, try **Conzelman Road** on the Marin Headlands; it overlooks bridge, Bay, and ocean. Take Alexander Street south under Highway 101 and wind up, up on the unmarked road for views that rival any in the world.

Fort Baker, established in 1897, is on the Marin edge just east of the bridge. You also take the Alexander Street turnoff, then follow signs to Fort Cronkhite, but—just before entering the tunnel—you turn right on Bunker Road. The U.S. Army has recently turned over administration of much of its 650 acres to the Golden Gate National Recreation Area. Up until then visitors could only enjoy the sea-level views back towards San Francisco and they could fish on the old military wharf or jetty at **Horseshoe Bay**. There wasn't much else. Plans call for scenic picnic areas, restoring the **natural beach** at this quiet crescent-shaped cove, and retaining the **boat launching ramp** east of the beach.

Sausalito

"Quiet, elegant, Mediterranean-like, an image that lingers," declares the **Sausalito** Chamber of Commerce. And, yes, there are many reasons—besides being minutes away from San Francisco by bridge or ferry—that tourists crowd into this Riviera. Whether you arrive by car, yacht, ferry, rented stretch Rolls Royce limousine, or bicycle, this cliffside village probably has what you're looking for.

Shopping? Downtown you can buy your way through dozens of galleries, boutiques, and craft or antique emporiums. Most, like the venerable **Village Fair**, are on or near Bridgeway, the scenic boulevard that hugs Richardson Bay. If you have the stamina to wind up all three stories of the Village Fair's Little Lombard, named after San Francisco's crookedest street, you can visit almost four dozen *shoppes* and artistic establishments and can often watch potters and silversmiths at work. Public rest-rooms on the mezzanine also lure you up.

Although its official population is under 7,000, Sausalito citizens had enough clout to narrowly defeat plans to run Highway 101's eight lanes along its priceless shoreline. Now, it's used for jogging, strolling, or just sitting to watch the sun's progress. Here, as almost everywhere in Sausalito, your eyes take in the masts of small boats, modest yachts, and full-rigged sailing boats; beyond the masts are Angel Island and that great, shining city at the other end of the Golden Gate Bridge. **Viewing is especially recommended at dusk** when San Francisco's skyline borrows the sunset's golds and reds and, as the hues fade, the lights of the city come on.

Downtown Bridgeway doesn't contain all the attractions. The shoreline has areas less well known. Don't miss Sausalito's imaginative and sometimes controversial **arks and houseboats** near Waldo Point on the north end. Houseboats are now required to attach plumbing pipes to shore and their tenants pay rent just like you or me. This is a far cry from the free-living days in the sixties when Zen philosopher Alan Watts and Varda, artist and catnip to women, occupied a half-rotted ferry among a tangle of boats housing other writers and artists, real or imagined. Now, besides a shrinking number of artistic types, the population includes developers, yachtsmen, store keepers, and a group labeled "hill snobs." How has this smorgasbord of people blended over the years? Often it hasn't.

In 1775, as they did at Angel Island, **Miwok Indians** watched Spanish explorer Juan Mañuel de Ayala discover *Saucelito*, which Ayala named for willows thriving by a stream. A later historic figure, enterprising English seaman **William Richardson**,

New plans are in the works for a beach and picnic facilities at Fort Baker.

married the daughter of the commandant of San Francisco's Presidio in 1825 and acquired the 19,000-acre Mexican land grant Rancho Saucelito. Richardson piloted boats, sold lumber, and barged barrels of fresh water to San Francisco. When Americans started competing for land and work, his earnings began to evaporate.

Around 1850 Richardson had to sell the southern portion of his ranch, which became known as **Old Town**. This took in Hurricane Gulch, subsequently renamed Shelter Cove (a more enticing name on real estate brochures). A few years later another historic event transpired, the opening of the oldest continually operating place of business in Sausalito. This pioneer enterprise was first called Walhalla Beer Garden, then the Valhalla restaurant when ex-madam Sally Stanford owned it. During her reign, the dining room decor included flower arrangements in toilet bowls. The Chart House chain, which has taken over, displays some items from that era.

In the early 1800s whalers—many of them Portuguese from the Azores—carried on their occupation from Shelter Cove. Over the years a sizable number of Portuguese settled in the flatlands. In the late spring their descendants still celebrate a colorful import from the Azores, the **Portuguese Chamarita** or Annual Holy Ghost and Pentecost Festival.

For many decades, starting in the 1890s, boisterous is too tame a word to describe life in the flats with its twenty-five bawdy houses, gambling dens, and saloons. In the meantime many Very English or Very Rich (including William Randolph Hearst) bought hillside estates, mainly in the **Banana Belt** or **New Town**. This privileged group could look down on the activity below, which continued during the lawless era of Prohibition.

Whether for better or worse, present life in downtown Sausalito is more tranquil. About the only hectic activity now is hunting for a parking place and then rushing back to cram more quarters into the meter. So—once your car has found a resting place near downtown Bridgeway—leave it and walk. You can usually find space to relax on benches in or near miniparks, piers, and along the seawall.

Besides boat-watching, this Bridgeway strand is great for people-watching. You'll see fellow visitors from all over the world; occasionally harbor seals may bob up near shore to watch the tourists. As for **fishing**, if you've brought a rod, why not join the eternal optimists trying their luck from the shore? This can be exciting during the very high tides between December and March when herring by the millions spawn. After the word gets out that the **herring run** is on, crowds of fishermen with dip nets line the shoreline. They are joined by flocks of happy seagulls who often stuff themselves so full of herring it takes hours before they can lift off the water.

Two Sausalito landmarks photographed by decades of visitors are within easy strolling distance of the ferry landing. Albert Sybrian's **bronze sea lion**, in the style of the Little Mermaid in Copenhagen, is a short distance south. North in the Plaza de Vina Del Mar Park is a pair of **fourteen-foot high elephants** sculpted for the Panama-Pacific Exposition.

Across the strand on the inland side the no name bar still carries on at 757 Bridgeway, but gone is the artistic ferment of the sixties when many considered Sausalito a suburb of the left bank of Paris. In fact, since tourists have taken over Bridgeway, townspeople conduct most of their business on Caledonia Street, which parallels Bridgeway; and a few craft and art shops have spilled over there, perhaps because parking is easier. Smitty's bar at 214 Caledonia—complete with pool table and pinball machine—

attracts some of the more colorful locals. Tuesday or Thursday at the **Sausalito Chamber of Commerce** (415/332-0505), 333 Caledonia, you can pick up tourist information.

Back to the waterfront, if you like an unprepossessing, nontouristy place to picnic, **Earl F. Dunphy Park** fits the bill with its tiny gazebo, grass, sand lot for kids, and a marsh being restored. Here you can watch water slosh up on the tiny beach next to the Sausalito Cruising Club barge. If you want to rent a sailboat or take **sailing lessons**, Cass' Rental Marina (415/332-6789) is adjacent.

Just to the north, beyond a parking lot with vehicles of uncertain years is a crowded gathering of boats in various states of repair. A sign identifies the area as the **Galilee Harbor** Tenant's Association. This may be the last stand of the bohemian-flower-children-live-on-boats-era. A fancy 194-berth marina is scheduled to go in to the north, and since developers are often eager, this boat community may have turned into concrete condos by the time you arrive.

The fascinating **Bay Model Visitor Center**, usually open Tuesday through Saturday from 9:00 A.M. to 4:00 P.M., is north at 2100 Bridgeway. Watch for signs and drive down the narrow road to the parking lot. There's a small picnic area, restrooms with a viewing platform on top, and the much-publicized tidal-hydraulic model of San Francisco Bay, its tributaries, and the Sacramento–San Joaquin River Delta.

This model has been of immense scientific value in searching for answers to complex hydrodynamic problems and to provide engineering data used to evaluate the possible impact of new projects in the Bay. It also shows where to clean up oil and chemical spills and how wastewater discharged into the Bay circulates. The U.S. Army Corps of Engineers, who built this scale model in the late fifties, admits that it doesn't look like the real thing. But is is almost two acres big and, when it is working, every 14.9 minutes two flood tides rush in under the six-foot Golden Gate Bridge and then ebb away. Even if the tides aren't turned on (call 415/332-3870 to check), the Center offers educational material and a film on the Bay.

Outside the big building where the model is housed is the North Pier, home to the Corps' debris boats that pick up tons of floatsam from the Bay each day. The Corps' dredges also call this home when they're not away helping keep the Bay navigable. The 204-foot-long *Wapama*, last of the coastal lumber carriers, sits on a barge here. After she dries out, the decision will be made whether she can be restored.

Look farther out past the long dock; You'll see what appears to be a rocky island with palm trees. Although the owner, Forbes Kiddo, calls it **Forbes Island**, this is actually a homemade houseboat with Captain Nemo–style underwater accommodations. It took Forbes over five years to construct his 400-ton barge-island, but for $2.5 million you can own it all. You can visit this fantasy island (for a hefty fee). Call 415/332-5727 between 9:00 A.M. and 5:00 P.M.

A SERIES OF GRASS-EDGED **yacht harbors** start just north of the Bay Model area. You can drive to the first on Marinship or walk along the **multi-use path** shared by joggers and bicyclists; the path continues to Mill Valley and on to western Marin or to Tiburon. Betwen the impressive yachts, you may see a few shorebirds foraging; there's a small sportfishing dock tucked into Clipper Yacht Harbor Basin 2.

On Harbor Drive, in a warren of commercial buildings, the bulky three-story Industrial Center Building contains studios where more than fifty working artists have taken refuge. These tenants, who work in many media—oil, watercolor, jewelry, posters, sculpture, and more—have an **art studio open house** the first weekend in December. For more details call the Academy Frame shop (415/332-9604). Many artists and artisans also show their work over the Labor Day weekend at the huge **Sausalito Art Festival**.

Waldo Point, where famous and infamous houseboats bobbed in the sixties, is actually outside the northern Sausalito boundary. Even farther north, the **houseboats and arks** now attached to shore at Kappa's Yacht Harbor are more sedate, whether they're small and fanciful or luxurious and all-decked-out. It's still worth driving in to envy this aquatic lifestyle where tenants are lulled by the rhythm of lapping water and hear the cries of gulls. But nothing is perfect; many a skylight is decorated with messages from those same gulls.

Just north of Sausalito, winged wildlife is often joined by small **seaplanes or helicopters** landing or taking off from the heliport at Commodore Seaplanes, Inc. (415/332-4843), on 242 Redwood Highway, actually in Mill Valley. If you want an impressive bird's eye view of San Francisco Bay or the coast, for a fee, take Highway 1 off 101, go east, and follow signs. There are also Champagne Sunset flights for the romantically inclined.

Forbes Island off the North Pier in Sausalito is actually a barge with dirt on it.

Where to eat in Sausalito? Along downtown Bridgeway almost every day as many as 500 people line up to grab one of thirty seats at Fred's Place for breakfast or lunch; others like the modestly priced Winships Restaurant and Sweet Shop (415/332-1454). If you like greenery, the Seven-Seas (415/332-1304) nearby offers a greenhouse atmosphere. Delis and ice cream shops are scattered along Bridgeway, and you can lunch at the Upstart Crow Coffee House (415/383-2084) in the basement of the bookstore at 749 Bridgeway. For modestly priced seafood with a view, try Flynn's Landing at 303 Johnson (415/332-0131). Zack's by the Bay (415/332-9779) at Bridgeway and Tourney features burgers and steaks.

At least once you should go all out and treat yourself to leisurely dining at the Bay's edge. Three choices are clustered on the 500 block of Bridgeway. The Ondine (415/332-0791) has served French and American cuisine for decades. Scoma's of Sausalito (there's also one at Larkspur Landing) advertises continental seafood (415/332-9551). The newer Horizons (415/331-3232) serves brunch daily until five. Farther north, the Spinnaker (415/332-1500) juts out into the bay and yachts often pass by just yards away outside the full-length windows.

Another restaurant with a four-star view is in the 1890 Alta Mira Hotel (415/332-1350), high in the hills at 125 Bulkley Avenue. If the weather cooperates, you can enjoy breakfast, lunch, and dinner outside as you gaze towards the Golden Gate and San Francisco. The thirty-two rooms, suites, and cottages of the Casa Madrona Hotel (415/332-0502) cling to the cliffside at 801 Bridgeway. Its restaurant, seven stories up, offers lunch and dinner plus **high tea** at 3 P.M. in flowered china pots along with mouth-watering pastries.

Where to stay? Sausalito has three hotels. Besides the Casa Madrona and Alta Mira, just mentioned, the Victorian-style Sausalito Hotel (415/332-4155) is by the Bay and ferry. Bed & Breakfast International (415/525-4569) has listings for **bed and breakfast** accommodations that range from private hillside homes to houseboats. There is a two-night minimum, which most guests find easy to bear.

That's about it, except for the Golden Gate **Youth Hostel** (415/331-2777) out on the Marin Headlands, where you can hobnob with owls, bobcats, and deer. They offer sixty bunks; most in dormitories. Hostel life is spartan and drinking alcohol is verboten. But the price is right and it's a great way to meet fellow vagabonds from around the world.

As you drive north from Sausalito on Highway 101 you glimpse small **Marin City**, where upwardly mobile suburbia is replacing boxlike World War II housing for Marinship workers. Unless you're headed for the **flea market** that starts before sunup on Saturdays and Sundays, you probably won't stop.

Mill Valley and Strawberry Peninsula

Next, cascading down the lower slopes of Mount Tamalpais, half-hidden in redwoods, is **Mill Valley.** And there was once an actual mill here. In Old Mill Park on Cascade Drive you can see the remains of the sawmill run by John Thomas Reed in the early 1800s.

Later, around the turn of the century, to escape the fog, many wealthy San Franciscans built summer homes here on streets with names like Morning Sun, Lark Lane, and Wisteria Way. Old-timers recall the crookedest railroad in the world that corkscrewed up Mount Tamalpais from 1896 to 1930, bringing thousands of city folk over for a day's jaunt.

Mill Valley still retains the look of a mountain resort, and the big annual event since 1905 is the **Dipsea Foot Race** to Stinson Beach over seven miles of rugged trails on Mount Tamalpais. Yet its residents enjoy a touch of the Bay, too.

As Highway 101 crosses the bridge over Richardson's Bay, below to the west you can see a **multipurpose trail** that runs across ninety-three acre **Bothin Marsh**. Besides bicyclists and joggers, you'll probably spot binocular-laden **birders**. The shorebirds have become so accustomed to the many bipeds, they often wander up close to this levee trail. To join them, take the Highway 1 turnoff towards Stinson Beach and park just off the highway near the Howard Johnson Motor Lodge. You can also connect with the multipurpose trail farther north off Miller Avenue, or at the north boundary of Sausalito.

Mill Valley's grassy **Bayside Park**, dedicated in 1984, boasts a small **fishing pier**, an exercise **parcourse**, and a **multipurpose trail**. The park is shared by egrets hunting food and healthy-looking dogs out for a romp. Finding the restrooms can be a challenge; they're hidden in the entrails of the sewage plant (called the Sewerage Agency of South Marin). Reaching Bayside Park is also a challenge. Turn north off Highway 1 at the Shoreline Drive exit at Almonte Boulevard, which becomes Miller Avenue; turn right on Camino Alto and again on Sycamore Avenue and continue past the school to the end. Good luck.

Strawberry Peninsula is on the east side of Highway 101 across from Mill Valley. To reach this enclave of wealthy homes, take the Tiburon Boulevard turnoff, turn right immediately on Frontage Road, and—if you can find your way through the traffic at the Town and Country Village Shopping Center—connect with Seminary Drive. A lagoon to your left, liked by birds, has some parking. About the only other place where you feel comfortable parking is on the scenic grounds of the **Golden Gate Baptist Theological Seminary**; just follow signs on and up. From there you can connect with the Great Circle Drive that loops around Strawberry Point to where you can see across Richardson Bay towards Sausalito and on to that city by the Golden Gate.

Once you return to Highway 101 and cross the Golden Gate Bridge, you're back where this book began. But don't stop there. You are sure to have found favorite places that you will visit again and again. Besides inevitable changes around the Bay's edge (hopefully more trails, parks, and marshes), there's always more to discover and rediscover. Even the Bay itself is transformed with each season and each hour.

So enjoy it again and again. After all, it is one of the wonders of the world.

A YEAR FULL of EVENTS

Here's a sampling of events all around the Bay. For more, contact the Chambers of Commerce listed in this book or call:

Fort Mason Center, San Francisco. Fifty resident groups and another 500 organizations put on enough events to keep you busy all year (415/441-5706).

East Bay Regional Parks offer a rich schedule of hikes and nature programs, especially at Coyote Hills, Crab Cove, and Tilden Park. (415/531-9300).

Candlestick Point State Recreational Area schedules kids' fishing lessons, bird walks, and other special events (415/557-4069 or 557-4127).

San Francisco Bay National Wildlife Refuge, Fremont, has many guided walks and nature programs. Recorded information, 415/792-3178 or phone 415/792-0222.

Fort Point hosts many special events. (415/556-1693).

JANUARY

It's the depths of winter, but the air is fresh and some flowers, like fragrant nosegays of sweet alyssum, are around.

New Year's Day Swim from Alcatraz to Aquatic Park, sponsored by the Sound End Rowing Club. Bundle up and watch from shore.

FEBRUARY

Chinese New Year (perhaps in late January) firecrackers and the big parade in Chinatown on a Saturday night. Check newspapers for specifics.

MARCH

In March golden poppies, purple lupine, and other wildflowers start their spring show. As they head north, ribbons of migrating birds stop briefly, and the mockingbird is heard.

Book Sale, usually mid-month, Fort Mason. Fantastic hardcover and paperback bargains; bring shopping bags. (415/558-3770).

APRIL

The wildflower displays continue to be spectacular, especially on the Marin Headlands and Angel Island.

Wildflower Show, first weekend, Oakland Museum (415/834-2413).

Opening Day of Yachting Season (last Sunday). Thousands of dressed-up boats parade from Tiburon to Sausalito to Fort Point and along the Marina and San Francisco waterfront. A must!

MAY

Summer is near when the hills turn brown (natives prefer calling them golden). Summer officially arrives on Memorial Day.

Portuguese Chamarita Holy Ghost Festival, Sunday six weeks after Easter, in Sausalito. Parade starts at 10 A.M., then free sopa and carne at Portuguese Hall, Caledonia and B streets.

Sand Castle/Sculpture Contest, Saturday in late May, Crown Memorial State Beach, Alameda. (415/531-9300).

Festival of the Wind, Saturday in late May, Coyote Hills Regional Park. (415/795-9385).

JUNE

Although it may hold off for a week or two, fog usually arrives; but, as mentioned, dress warmly and fog is not a four-letter word.

Festival of the Lake (first weekend, probably), Lake Merritt, Oakland. Hundreds of performers, food, booths. (415/893-0677).

JULY

The fog thickens. Mark Twain is often quoted as saying, "the coldest winter I ever spent was one summer in San Francisco."

July Fourth Fireworks explode around the Bay, but the big show—when darkness falls—is at Crissy Field, San Francisco, preceded by hours of music and entertainment. 415/556-0560 or 556-4460.

Solano County Fair, mid-July in Vallejo.

AUGUST

Wild blackberries are ripe. That gray air conditioner is still around, but the sun may make an appearance, even on a weekend.

Marin County Fair, first weekend, Civic Center Fairground, San Rafael.

ACC Crafts Fair, mid-month, Fort Mason. Crafts from across the United States.

SEPTEMBER

The Bay's real summer begins around Labor Day, usually. Summer fog may retreat for days while the weather turns soft and balmy. Hundreds of hawks head south over the Golden Gate.

Sausalito Art Festival, over Labor Day weekend. A biggie!

San Francisco Blues Festival, mid-month, Fort Mason.

OCTOBER

Perhaps Indian summer arrives.

Blessing of the Fishing Fleet, first Sunday, noonish. Parade from St. Peter and Paul's down Columbus Avenue to Fisherman's Wharf.

Columbus Day Celebration, Sunday. Big afternoon parade through the city to North Beach; events the day before at Aquatic Park.

Whaleboat Regatta, late October in Vallejo. Sponsored by the California Maritime Academy. (707/643-7542).

S.F. Fall Antiques Show, late October or early November, Fort Mason.

NOVEMBER

Most birds have headed south. The rains get down to serious business. But there are occasional days so balmy you can eat Thanksgiving dinner outside at a shoreline park.

DECEMBER

It's brrrisk, probably rainy, so why not view Yule decorations along San Francisco's Marina Boulevard from your car? Or enjoy Christmas color and cheer inside at Ghirardelli Square, The Cannery, Pier 39, and in the shops of Sausalito.

Art studio open house, first weekend in December. Sausalito's Industrial Center Building, which houses fifty working artists.

Guardsmen Christmas Tree Sale, starts early in month, Fort Mason.

INDEX

*Pick your interest and location, go to it,
and enjoy!*

Historic China Camp where you can picnic, wade, swim and enjoy the local shrimp cocktails.